Working Papers for
Exercises and Problems
Chapters 1-16

Principles of Accounting
and
Principles of Financial Accounting
Twelfth Edition

Belverd E. Needles, Jr., Ph.D., C.P.A., C.M.A.
DePaul University

Marian Powers, Ph.D.
Northwestern University

Susan V. Crosson, M.S. Accounting, C.P.A.
Emory University

SOUTH-WESTERN
CENGAGE Learning

Australia • Brazil • Japan • Korea • Mexico • Singapore • Spain • United Kingdom • United States

For product information and technology assistance, contact us at **Cengage Learning Academic Resource Center, 1-800-423-0563**.

For permission to use material from this text or product, submit all requests online at **www.cengage.com/permissions**. Further permissions questions can be emailed to **permissionrequest@cengage.com**.

ISBN-13: 978-1-133-96245-8
ISBN-10: 1-133-96245-9

South-Western Cengage Learning
5191 Natorp Boulevard
Mason, OH 45040
USA

Cengage Learning is a leading provider of customized learning solutions with office locations around the globe, including Singapore, the United Kingdom, Australia, Mexico, Brazil, and Japan. Locate your local office at: **international.cengage.com/region**.

Cengage Learning products are represented in Canada by Nelson Education, Ltd.

For your course and learning solutions, visit **www.cengage.com**.

Purchase any of our products at your local college store or at our preferred online store **www.CengageBrain.com**.

Printed in the United States of America
1 2 3 4 5 6 7   17 16 15 14 13

CONTENTS

Chapter

Note to Students

This book contains Working Papers to be used in preparing solutions to all Exercises and Problems in Chapters 1-16 of *Principles of Accounting* and *Principles of Financial Accounting,* Twelfth Edition. The Working Papers are designed to simplify your work. Appropriate forms for computational assignments for each exercise and problem are provided, and some preliminary information has been printed to get you started.

Accounting Format Guide

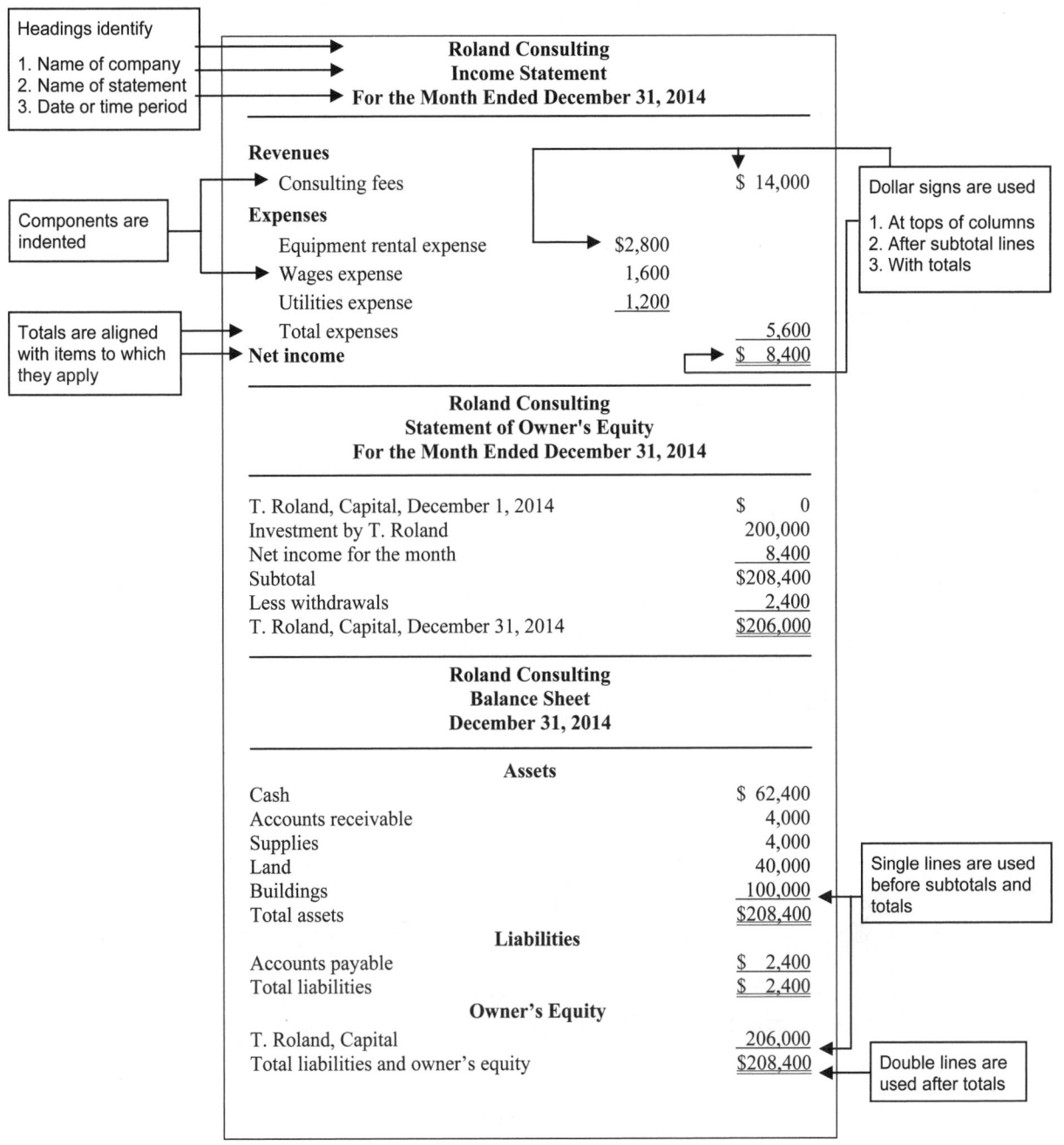

Headings identify
1. Name of company
2. Name of statement
3. Date or time period

Components are indented

Totals are aligned with items to which they apply

Roland Consulting
Income Statement
For the Month Ended December 31, 2014

Revenues		
Consulting fees		$ 14,000
Expenses		
Equipment rental expense	$2,800	
Wages expense	1,600	
Utilities expense	1,200	
Total expenses		5,600
Net income		$ 8,400

Dollar signs are used
1. At tops of columns
2. After subtotal lines
3. With totals

Roland Consulting
Statement of Owner's Equity
For the Month Ended December 31, 2014

T. Roland, Capital, December 1, 2014	$ 0
Investment by T. Roland	200,000
Net income for the month	8,400
Subtotal	$208,400
Less withdrawals	2,400
T. Roland, Capital, December 31, 2014	$206,000

Roland Consulting
Balance Sheet
December 31, 2014

Assets	
Cash	$ 62,400
Accounts receivable	4,000
Supplies	4,000
Land	40,000
Buildings	100,000
Total assets	$208,400
Liabilities	
Accounts payable	$ 2,400
Total liabilities	$ 2,400
Owner's Equity	
T. Roland, Capital	206,000
Total liabilities and owner's equity	$208,400

Single lines are used before subtotals and totals

Double lines are used after totals

ACCOUNTING PRINCIPLES AND THE FINANCIAL STATEMENTS

Short Exercises

SE1. Accounting Concepts

1.		4.	
2.		5.	
3.			

SE2. Forms of Business Organization

1.		4.	
2.		5.	
3.		6.	

SE3. The Accounting Equation

1.	Assets	=	
2.	Owner's Equity	=	
3.	Liabilities	=	

SE4. The Accounting Equation

1.	Assets	=	Liabilities	+	Owner's Equity		
		=		+	Owner's Equity		
		–		=			
	Owner's Equity	=					
2.	Assets	=	Assets	+			
	Assets –	Assets	=				
		Assets	=				
		Assets	=		/		
		Assets	=				
		Liabilities	=		×		=

SE5. The Accounting Equation

1.	Beginning:		=	Liabilities	+	
		Liabilities	=			
			=		+	
	Change:					
			=		+	Owner's Equity
	End:	Owner's Equity	=			
2.	Beginning:	Assets	=		+	
		Assets	=			
			=		+	
	Change:					
			=		+	Owner's Equity
	End:	Owner's Equity	=			

SE6. The Accounting Equation and Net Income

	Net income	=	
Beginning of year:			
Assets	=	Liabilities	+	Owner's Equity	
	=		+	
During year:			
	Investment		
	Withdrawals		
	Net Income		
End of year:			
	=		+	

SE7. Preparation and Completion of a Balance Sheet

Assets		Liabilities	
		Owner's Equity	

SE8. Preparation of Financial Statements

Assets		Liabilities	
		Owner's Equity	

SE9. Accounting and Business Enterprises

1.		6.	
2.		7.	
3.		8.	
4.		9.	
5.		10.	

SE 10. Ethics and Accounting

1.		3.	
2.		4.	

Exercises: Set A

E1A. Business Transactions

1.	
2.	
3.	
4.	

E2A. Accounting Concepts

1.		6.	
2.		7.	
3.		8.	
4.		9.	
5.		10.	

E3A. Money Measure

Company	Sales			
		×	=	
		×	=	
		×	=	
		×	=	

Company	Assets			
		×	=	
		×	=	
		×	=	
		×	=	

E4A. The Accounting Equation

1.		Assets	=	Liabilities	+	Owner's Equity
			=	Liabilities	+	
		Liabilities	=			

2.		Assets	=	Liabilities	+	Owner's Equity
		Assets	=		+	
		Assets	=			

3.		Assets	=		+	
		2/3 Assets	=			
		Assets	=			
		Liabilities	=		×	=

4.	Beginning:		=	Liabilities	+	
		Liabilities	=			
			=		+	
	Change:					
			=		+	Owner's Equity
	End:	Owner's Equity	=			

E5A. Owner's Equity and the Accounting Equation

1.						
			Assets	=	Liabilities	+	Owner's Equity
				=		+	
				=		+	

2.						

3.						

4.						

E6A. Identification of Accounts

1.	a.		2.	a.	
	b.			b.	
	c.			c.	
	d.			d.	
	e.			e.	
	f.			f.	
	g.			g.	

E7A. Preparation of a Balance Sheet

Assets		Liabilities	
		Owner's Equity	

E8A. Preparation and Integration of Financial Statements

Assets		Liabilities	
		Owner's Equity	

E9A. Statement of Cash Flows

E10A. Statement of Owner's Equity

E11A. Preparation and Integration of Financial Statements

E12A. Users of Accounting Information and Forms of Business Organization

E13A. The Nature of Accounting

1.		5.		9.	
2.		6.		10.	
3.		7.		11.	
4.		8.		12.	

E14A. Accounting Abbreviations

CPA:	
IRS:	
PCAOB:	
GAAP:	
FASB:	
SEC:	
GASB:	
IASB:	
IMA:	
AICPA:	

E15A. Ethics and Accounting

1.	
2.	
3.	
4.	
5.	

Problems

P1. Preparation and Interpretation of Financial Statements

1.

Utilities expense		Accounts payable
Building		Rent expense
Owner's capital		Withdrawals
Net income		Fees earned
Land		Cash
Equipment		Supplies
Revenues		Wages expense
Accounts receivable		

2.

P2. Integration of Financial Statements

1.

	Set A		Set B		Set C	
Income Statement						
Statement of Owner's Equity						
Balance Sheet						

2.

P3. Preparation and Interpretation of Financial Statements

1.

Assets

Liabilities

Owner's Equity

2.

P4. Preparation and Interpretation of Financial Statements

1.

	Assets		Liabilities	

		Owner's Equity	

2.

P5. Use and Interpretation of Financial Statements

1.

2.

3.

4.

Alternate Problems

P6. Preparation and Interpretation of Financial Statements

1.

Wages expense		Accounts payable
Equipment		Rent expense
Equipment rental expense		Withdrawals
Net income		Fees earned
Land		Cash
Owner's capital		Supplies
Revenues		Utilities expense
Accounts receivable		

2.

P7. Integration of Financial Statements

1.

	Set A		Set B		Set C	
Income Statement						
Statement of Owner's Equity						
Balance Sheet						

2.

P8. Preparation and Interpretation of Financial Statements

1.

Assets		Liabilities		
		Owner's Equity		

2.

P9. Preparation and Interpretation of Financial Statements

1.

	Assets		Liabilities		
			Owner's Equity		

2.

P10. Use and Interpretation of Financial Statements

1.

2.

3.

4.

CHAPTER 2—Working Papers

ANALYZING AND RECORDING BUSINESS TRANSACTIONS

Short Exercises

SE1. Classification of Accounts

a.		e.	
b.		f.	
c.		g.	
d.		h.	

SE2. Recognition, Valuation, and Classification

SE3. Recognition

SE4. Normal Balances

a.		e.	
b.		f.	
c.		g.	
d.		h.	

SE5. Transaction Analysis

May	2	
	5	
	7	
	19	
	22	
	25	
	31	

SE6. Recording Transactions in T Accounts

SE7. Preparing a Trial Balance

SE8. Recording Transactions in the General Journal

	General Journal				Page 4
Date	Description	Post. Ref.	Debit	Credit	

SE9. Posting to the Ledger Accounts

Cash					Account No.	
					Balance	
Date	Item	Post. Ref.	Debit	Credit	Debit	Credit

Accounts Receivable					Account No.	
					Balance	
Date	Item	Post. Ref.	Debit	Credit	Debit	Credit

Service Revenue					Account No.	
					Balance	
Date	Item	Post. Ref.	Debit	Credit	Debit	Credit

Note: At this point, the account numbers would also be posted to the accounts in the general journal in SE8.

2-4

SE10. Recording Transactions in the General Journal

General Journal

Date	Description	Post. Ref.	Debit	Credit

SE11. Identifying Ethical Transactions

1	
2	
3	

SE12. Timing and Cash Flows

Cash

Exercises: Set A

E1A. Recognition

E2A. T Accounts, Normal Balance, and the Accounting Equation

E3A. Classification of Accounts

Item	Asset	Liability	Owner's Equity D. Minimus, Capital	Owner's Equity D. Minimus, Withdrawals	Revenue	Expense	Normal Balance Debit	Normal Balance Credit
a.								
b.								
c.								
d.								
e.								
f.								
g.								
h.								
i.								
j.								
k.								
l.								
m.								
n.								
o.								
p.								
q.								
r.								
s.								
t.								
u.								
v.								
w.								
x.								

E4A. Transaction Analysis

a.

b.

c.

d.

e.

f.

g.

E5A. Transaction Analysis

		Debit	Credit
a.	Paid for supplies purchased on credit last month.	5	1
b.	Received cash from customers billed last month.		
c.	Made a payment on accounts payable.		
d.	Purchased supplies on credit.		
e.	Billed a customer for lawn services.		
f.	Made a rent payment for the current month.		
g.	Received cash from customers for repair services.		
h.	Paid employee wages.		
i.	Ordered equipment.		
j.	Received and paid for the equipment ordered in *i*.		

E6A. Recording Transactions in T Accounts

E7A. Analysis of Transactions

a.	
b.	
c.	
d.	
e.	
f.	
g.	
h.	

E8A. Analysis of Unfamiliar Transactions

E9A. Trial Balance

E10A. Preparing a Trial Balance

E11A. Effects of Errors on a Trial Balance

a.	
b.	
c.	
d.	

E12A. Correcting Errors in a Trial Balance

E13A. Recording Transactions in the General Journal

General Journal

2014					
	a.				
	b.				
	c.				
	d.				
	e.				
	f.				
	g.				
	h.				

E14A. Recording Transactions in the General Journal and Posting to the Ledger Accounts

General Journal

Page 10

Date	Description	Post. Ref.	Debit	Credit

General Ledger

Cash

Account No.

Date	Item	Post. Ref.	Debit	Credit	Balance Debit	Balance Credit

Office Equipment

Account No.

Date	Item	Post. Ref.	Debit	Credit	Balance Debit	Balance Credit

Accounts Payable

Account No.

Date	Item	Post. Ref.	Debit	Credit	Balance Debit	Balance Credit

E15A. Application of Recognition Point

1. Purchases recognized on date shipped

Order	Date Shipped	Date Received	Amount	

2. Purchases recognized on date received

Order	Date Shipped	Date Received	Amount	

E16A. Cash Flow Analysis

2-15

Problems

P1. T Accounts, Normal Balance, and The Accounting Equation

Assets	=	Liabilities	+	Owner's Equity				
				R. Mehta, Capital	−	R. Mehta, Withdrawals	+	Revenues	−	Expenses

| Cash | | Accounts Payable | | R. Mehta, Capital | | R. Mehta, Withdrawals | | Design Revenue | | Rent Expense |

| Accounts Receivable | | Loans Payable | | | | | | | | Telephone Expense |

| Equipment | | Unearned Revenue | | | | | | | | Wages Expense |

Accounting equation without Equipment:

| Equipment | + | | = |
| Equipment | | | = |

Accounting equation in balance:

| | = | | + | |
| | = | |

P2. Transaction Analysis

		Debit	Credit
a.	Paid for supplies purchased on credit last month.	7	1
b.	Received a bill for repairs.		
c.	Paid the current month's rent.		
d.	Purchased supplies on credit.		
e.	Received cash from customers for services performed but not yet billed.		
f.	Purchased equipment on account.		
g.	Billed customers for services performed.		
h.	Returned part of the equipment purchased in *f* for a credit.		
i.	Received payments from customers previously billed.		
j.	Paid the bill received in *b*.		
k.	Received an order for services to be performed.		
l.	Paid for repairs with cash.		
m.	Made a payment to reduce the principal of the note payable.		
n.	Made a cash withdrawal.		

3.

4.

P4. Transaction Analysis, Journal Form, T Accounts, and Trial Balance

1.

3.

4.

P5. Transaction Analysis, General Journal, Ledger Accounts, and Trial Balance

3. (Requirements 1, 2, 4, and 5 follow)

	General Journal			Page 22
Date	**Description**	**Post. Ref.**	**Debit**	**Credit**

1, 2, and 4.

					Account No.	
		Post.			Balance	
Date	Item	Ref.	Debit	Credit	Debit	Credit

					Account No.	
		Post.			Balance	
Date	Item	Ref.	Debit	Credit	Debit	Credit

					Account No.	
		Post.			Balance	
Date	Item	Ref.	Debit	Credit	Debit	Credit

					Account No.	
		Post.			Balance	
Date	Item	Ref.	Debit	Credit	Debit	Credit

P5. Transaction Analysis, General Journal, Ledger Accounts, and Trial Balance (Continued)

					Account No.	
					Balance	
		Post.			Debit	Credit
Date	**Item**	**Ref.**	**Debit**	**Credit**	**Debit**	**Credit**

					Account No.	
					Balance	
		Post.			Debit	Credit
Date	**Item**	**Ref.**	**Debit**	**Credit**	**Debit**	**Credit**

					Account No.	
					Balance	
		Post.			Debit	Credit
Date	**Item**	**Ref.**	**Debit**	**Credit**	**Debit**	**Credit**

					Account No.	
					Balance	
		Post.			Debit	Credit
Date	**Item**	**Ref.**	**Debit**	**Credit**	**Debit**	**Credit**

					Account No.	
					Balance	
		Post.			Debit	Credit
Date	**Item**	**Ref.**	**Debit**	**Credit**	**Debit**	**Credit**

					Account No.	
					Balance	
		Post.			Debit	Credit
Date	**Item**	**Ref.**	**Debit**	**Credit**	**Debit**	**Credit**

2-25

P5. **Transaction Analysis, General Journal, Ledger Accounts, and Trial Balance** (Continued)

					Account No.	
					Balance	
Date	**Item**	**Post. Ref.**	**Debit**	**Credit**	**Debit**	**Credit**

					Account No.	
					Balance	
Date	**Item**	**Post. Ref.**	**Debit**	**Credit**	**Debit**	**Credit**

5.

6.

Alternate Problems

P6. T Accounts, Normal Balance, and the Accounting Equation

Assets	=	Liabilities	+	Owner's Equity						
				B. Carlson, Capital	−	B. Carlson, Withdrawals	+	Revenues	−	Expenses

Accounting equation without Cash:

Cash	+		=			
		Cash	=			

Accounting equation in balance:

	=		+	
	=			

		Debit	Credit
P7.	**Transaction Analysis**		
a.	Paid for supplies purchased on credit last month.	7	1
b.	Billed customers for services performed.		
c.	Paid the current month's rent.		
d.	Purchased supplies on credit.		
e.	Received cash from customers for services performed but not yet billed.		
f.	Purchased equipment on account.		
g.	Received a bill for repairs.		
h.	Returned part of the equipment purchased in *f* for a credit.		
i.	Received payments from customers previously billed.		
j.	Paid the bill received in *g*.		
k.	Received an order for services to be performed.		
l.	Paid for repairs with cash.		
m.	Made a payment to reduce the principal of the note payable.		
n.	Made a cash withdrawal.		

P8. Transaction Analysis, T Accounts, and Trial Balance

1 and 2.

P8. Transaction Analysis, T Accounts, and Trial Balance (Concluded)

3.

4.

© 2014 Cengage Learning. All Rights Reserved. May not be scanned, copied, duplicated, or posted to a publicly accessible website, in whole or in part.

P9. Transaction Analysis, T Accounts, and Trial Balances

1 and 2.

3.

4.

P10. Transaction Analysis, General Journal, Ledger Accounts, and Trial Balance

3. (Requirements 1, 2, 4, 5, and 6 follow)

		General Journal			Page 17
Date		Description	Post. Ref.	Debit	Credit

P10. Transaction Analysis, General Journal, Ledger Accounts, and Trial Balance (Continued)

	General Journal			Page 18
Date	**Description**	**Post. Ref.**	**Debit**	**Credit**

P10. Transaction Analysis, General Journal, Ledger Accounts, and Trial Balance (Continued)

P10. Transaction Analysis, General Journal, Ledger Accounts, and Trial Balance (Continued)

1, 2, and 4.

Cash

Date	Item	Post. Ref.	Debit	Credit	Balance Debit	Credit

Account No.

Date	Item	Post. Ref.	Debit	Credit	Balance Debit	Credit

Account No.

Date	Item	Post. Ref.	Debit	Credit	Balance Debit	Credit

Account No.

Date	Item	Post. Ref.	Debit	Credit	Balance Debit	Credit

					Account No.	
		Post.			Balance	
Date	Item	Ref.	Debit	Credit	Debit	Credit

					Account No.	
		Post.			Balance	
Date	Item	Ref.	Debit	Credit	Debit	Credit

					Account No.	
		Post.			Balance	
Date	Item	Ref.	Debit	Credit	Debit	Credit

					Account No.	
		Post.			Balance	
Date	Item	Ref.	Debit	Credit	Debit	Credit

					Account No.	
		Post.			Balance	
Date	Item	Ref.	Debit	Credit	Debit	Credit

					Account No.	
		Post.			Balance	
Date	Item	Ref.	Debit	Credit	Debit	Credit

P10. Transaction Analysis, General Journal, Ledger Accounts, and Trial Balance (Continued)

					Account No.	
		Post.			**Balance**	
Date	**Item**	**Ref.**	**Debit**	**Credit**	**Debit**	**Credit**

					Account No.	
		Post.			**Balance**	
Date	**Item**	**Ref.**	**Debit**	**Credit**	**Debit**	**Credit**

					Account No.	
		Post.			**Balance**	
Date	**Item**	**Ref.**	**Debit**	**Credit**	**Debit**	**Credit**

					Account No.	
		Post.			**Balance**	
Date	**Item**	**Ref.**	**Debit**	**Credit**	**Debit**	**Credit**

5.

6.

CHAPTER 3—Working Papers
ADJUSTING THE ACCOUNTS

Short Exercises

SE1. Accrual Accounting Concepts

1.	
2.	
3.	
4.	

SE2. Adjustment for Prepaid Insurance

				+		−		=			

SE3. Adjustment for Supplies

				+		−		=			

SE4. Adjustment for Depreciation

SE5. Adjustment for Accrued Wages

			(	/	) ×		=			

SE6. Adjustment for Unearned Revenue

SE7. Preparation of an Income Statement and Statement of Owner's Equity from an Adjusted Trial Balance

SE8. Preparation of an Income Statement and Statement of Owner's Equity from an Adjusted Trial Balance

SE9. Determination of Cash Flows

SE10. Determination of Cash Flows

Exercises: Set A

E1A. Applications of Accounting Concepts Related to Accrual Accounting

1.	
2.	
3.	
4.	
5.	
6.	

E2A. Application of Conditions for Revenue Recognition

a.	
b.	
c.	
d.	

E3A. Adjusting Entry for Unearned Revenue

E4A. Adjusting Entries for Prepaid Insurance

1.					
		−	=		
2.					

E5A. Adjusting Entries for Supplies: Missing Data

1.

	a	b	c	d

2.

E6A. Adjusting Entry for Accrued Salaries

1.

		$/$ $=$ $\times$		
	$=$		

2.

E7A. Revenue and Expense Recognition

1.

$($ $\times$ $)$	

2.

E8A. Accounting for Revenue Received in Advance

1.

		(	/	)	
		×	=		

2.

E9A. Adjusting Entries

1.

	+		
	=		
	−		

2.

3.

4.

5.

6.

Assets

Liabilities

Owner's Equity

E11A. Determination of Cash Flows

E12A. Relationship of Expenses to Cash Paid

1.

2.

3.

Problems

P1. Determining Adjustments

	Balance Sheet Account	Amount of Adjustment (+ or −)	Balance after Adjustment	Income Statement Account	Amount of Adjustment (+ or −)	Balance after Adjustment
a.		−			+	
b.		−			+	
c.		+			+	
d.		−			+	
e.		+			+	

P2. Preparing Adjusting Entries

1.

a.							
				+		−	
		=					

b.							
			[(		/	)	
		×		]			
			[(		/	)	
		×		]			

c.

d.

			(		/	)	
		×		=			

e.

f.

g.							
			(		/	)	
		×		=			

h.

2.

P3. Determining Adjusting Entries, Posting to T Accounts, and Preparing an Adjusted Trial Balance

1. and 2.

P3. Determining Adjusting Entries, Posting to T Accounts, and Preparing an Adjusted Trial Balance (Concluded)

3.

4.

a.

b.

c.

d.

e.

f.

g.

P4. Determining Adjusting Entries and Tracing Their Effects to Financial Statements

1.

	General Journal				Page 14
Date	**Description**	**Post. Ref.**	**Debit**	**Credit**	
	− =				
	× =				
	− =				

P4. Determining Adjusting Entries and Tracing Their Effects to Financial Statements (Continued)

2. and 3.

Cash   **Account No.**

Date	Item	Post. Ref.	Debit	Credit	Balance Debit	Balance Credit

Accounts Receivable   **Account No.**

Date	Item	Post. Ref.	Debit	Credit	Balance Debit	Balance Credit

Prepaid Rent   **Account No.**

Date	Item	Post. Ref.	Debit	Credit	Balance Debit	Balance Credit

Prepaid Insurance   **Account No.**

Date	Item	Post. Ref.	Debit	Credit	Balance Debit	Balance Credit

Prepaid Maintenance   **Account No.**

Date	Item	Post. Ref.	Debit	Credit	Balance Debit	Balance Credit

Spare Parts   **Account No.**

Date	Item	Post. Ref.	Debit	Credit	Balance Debit	Balance Credit

P4. **Determining Adjusting Entries and Tracing Their Effects to Financial Statements**
(Continued)

Limousines Account No. _____

Date	Item	Post. Ref.	Debit	Credit	Balance Debit	Balance Credit

Accumulated Depreciation—Limousines Account No. _____

Date	Item	Post. Ref.	Debit	Credit	Balance Debit	Balance Credit

Notes Payable Account No. _____

Date	Item	Post. Ref.	Debit	Credit	Balance Debit	Balance Credit

Unearned Passenger Service Revenue Account No. _____

Date	Item	Post. Ref.	Debit	Credit	Balance Debit	Balance Credit

Interest Payable Account No. _____

Date	Item	Post. Ref.	Debit	Credit	Balance Debit	Balance Credit

A. Phylum, Capital Account No. _____

Date	Item	Post. Ref.	Debit	Credit	Balance Debit	Balance Credit

P4. Determining Adjusting Entries and Tracing Their Effects to Financial Statements
(Continued)

A. Phylum, Withdrawals

Account No.

Date	Item	Post. Ref.	Debit	Credit	Balance Debit	Balance Credit

Passenger Service Revenue

Account No.

Date	Item	Post. Ref.	Debit	Credit	Balance Debit	Balance Credit

Gas and Oil Expense

Account No.

Date	Item	Post. Ref.	Debit	Credit	Balance Debit	Balance Credit

Salaries Expense

Account No.

Date	Item	Post. Ref.	Debit	Credit	Balance Debit	Balance Credit

Advertising Expense

Account No.

Date	Item	Post. Ref.	Debit	Credit	Balance Debit	Balance Credit

Rent Expense

Account No.

Date	Item	Post. Ref.	Debit	Credit	Balance Debit	Balance Credit

Insurance Expense

Account No.

Date	Item	Post. Ref.	Debit	Credit	Balance Debit	Balance Credit

Spare Parts Expense   Account No.

Date	Item	Post. Ref.	Debit	Credit	Balance Debit	Balance Credit

Depreciation Expense—Limousines   Account No.

Date	Item	Post. Ref.	Debit	Credit	Balance Debit	Balance Credit

Maintenance Expense   Account No.

Date	Item	Post. Ref.	Debit	Credit	Balance Debit	Balance Credit

Interest Expense   Account No.

Date	Item	Post. Ref.	Debit	Credit	Balance Debit	Balance Credit

P4. Determining Adjusting Entries and Tracing Their Effects to Financial Statements
(Continued)

4.

Note: Prepaid Rent does not appear on the adjusted trial balance because it now has a zero balance.

P4. Determining Adjusting Entries and Tracing Their Effects to Financial Statements (Concluded)

Assets

Liabilities

Owner's Equity

5.

P5. Determining Adjustments

	Balance Sheet Account	Amount of Adjustment (+ or −)	Balance after Adjustment	Income Statement Account	Amount of Adjustment (+ or −)	Balance after Adjustment
a.		−			+	
b.		−			+	
c.		+				
d.		+			+	
e.		−			+	
f.		+			+	

P6. Determining Adjusting Entries, Posting to T Accounts, and Preparing an Adjusted Trial Balance

1. and 2.

P6. Determining Adjusting Entries, Posting to T Accounts, and Preparing an Adjusted Trial Balance (Concluded)

3.

4.

a.
b.
c.
d.
e.
f.
g.

P7. Preparing Adjusting Entries

1.

a.								

b.

$$(\quad / \quad)$$
$$\times \quad = $$

c.

d.

$$+ \quad - $$

e.

$$[(\quad / \quad)$$
$$\times \quad]$$
$$[(\quad / \quad)$$
$$\times \quad]$$

f.

g.

$$(\quad / \quad)$$
$$\times \quad = $$

h.

2.

1. and 2.

P8. Determining Adjusting Entries and Tracing Their Effects to Financial Statements
(Continued)

3.

Note: Unearned Tax Fees does not appear on the adjusted trial balance because it now has a zero balance.

P8. Determining Adjusting Entries and Tracing Their Effects to Financial Statements (Concluded)

Assets		

Liabilities		

Owner's Equity		

4.

Alternate Problems

P9. Determining Adjustments

Balance Sheet Account	Amount of Adjustment (+ or −)	Balance after Adjustment	Income Statement Account	Amount of Adjustment (+ or −)	Balance after Adjustment
a.	−			+	
b.	−			+	
c.	+				
d.	−			+	
e.	+			+	

P10. Preparing Adjusting Entries

1.

a.								
				+		−		
		=						

b.								
				[(		/	)	
				×		]		
				[(		/	)	
				×		]		

c.								

d.								
				(		/	)	
		×		=				

e.								

f.								

g.								
				(		/	) ×	
				=				

h.								

2.

P11. Determining Adjusting Entries, Posting to T Accounts, and Preparing an Adjusted Trial Balance

1. and 2.

P11. Determining Adjusting Entries, Posting to T Accounts, and Preparing an Adjusted Trial Balance (Concluded)

3.

4.	**a.**	
	b.	
	c.	
	d.	
	e.	
	f.	
	g.	

P12. Determining Adjusting Entries and Tracing Their Effects to Financial Statements

1.

		General Journal				Page 14
Date		**Description**	**Post. Ref.**	**Debit**		**Credit**
		− =				
		× =				
		− =				

P12. Determining Adjusting Entries and Tracing Their Effects to Financial Statements
(Continued)

2. and 3.

Cash | | | | | **Account No.**

Date	Item	Post. Ref.	Debit	Credit	Balance Debit	Balance Credit

Accounts Receivable | | | | | **Account No.**

Date	Item	Post. Ref.	Debit	Credit	Balance Debit	Balance Credit

Prepaid Rent | | | | | **Account No.**

Date	Item	Post. Ref.	Debit	Credit	Balance Debit	Balance Credit

Prepaid Insurance | | | | | **Account No.**

Date	Item	Post. Ref.	Debit	Credit	Balance Debit	Balance Credit

Prepaid Maintenance | | | | | **Account No.**

Date	Item	Post. Ref.	Debit	Credit	Balance Debit	Balance Credit

Spare Parts | | | | | **Account No.**

Date	Item	Post. Ref.	Debit	Credit	Balance Debit	Balance Credit

P12. Determining Adjusting Entries and Tracing Their Effects to Financial Statements
(Continued)

Cars Account No.

Date	Item	Post. Ref.	Debit	Credit	Balance Debit	Balance Credit

Accumulated Depreciation—Cars Account No.

Date	Item	Post. Ref.	Debit	Credit	Balance Debit	Balance Credit

Notes Payable Account No.

Date	Item	Post. Ref.	Debit	Credit	Balance Debit	Balance Credit

Unearned Rental Service Revenue Account No.

Date	Item	Post. Ref.	Debit	Credit	Balance Debit	Balance Credit

Interest Payable Account No.

Date	Item	Post. Ref.	Debit	Credit	Balance Debit	Balance Credit

S. Navarro, Capital Account No.

Date	Item	Post. Ref.	Debit	Credit	Balance Debit	Balance Credit

P12. Determining Adjusting Entries and Tracing Their Effects to Financial Statements
(Continued)

S. Navarro, Withdrawals   Account No.

Date	Item	Post. Ref.	Debit	Credit	Balance Debit	Balance Credit

Rental Service Revenue   Account No.

Date	Item	Post. Ref.	Debit	Credit	Balance Debit	Balance Credit

Gas and Oil Expense   Account No.

Date	Item	Post. Ref.	Debit	Credit	Balance Debit	Balance Credit

Salaries Expense   Account No.

Date	Item	Post. Ref.	Debit	Credit	Balance Debit	Balance Credit

Advertising Expense   Account No.

Date	Item	Post. Ref.	Debit	Credit	Balance Debit	Balance Credit

Rent Expense   Account No.

Date	Item	Post. Ref.	Debit	Credit	Balance Debit	Balance Credit

Insurance Expense

Account No.

Date	Item	Post. Ref.	Debit	Credit	Balance Debit	Balance Credit

Spare Parts Expense

Account No.

Date	Item	Post. Ref.	Debit	Credit	Balance Debit	Balance Credit

Depreciation Expense—Cars

Account No.

Date	Item	Post. Ref.	Debit	Credit	Balance Debit	Balance Credit

Maintenance Expense

Account No.

Date	Item	Post. Ref.	Debit	Credit	Balance Debit	Balance Credit

Interest Expense

Account No.

Date	Item	Post. Ref.	Debit	Credit	Balance Debit	Balance Credit

P12. Determining Adjusting Entries and Tracing Their Effects to Financial Statements (Continued)

4.

Note: Prepaid Rent does not appear on the adjusted trial balance because it now has a zero balance.

P12. Determining Adjusting Entries and Tracing Their Effects to Financial Statements
(Concluded)

Assets

Liabilities

Owner's Equity

5.

P13. Determining Adjustments

	Balance Sheet Account	Amount of Adjustment (+ or −)	Balance after Adjustment	Income Statement Account	Amount of Adjustment (+ or −)	Balance after Adjustment
a.		−			+	
b.		−			+	
c.		+			+	
d.		+			+	
e.		+			+	
f.		−			+	

P14. Determining Adjusting Entries, Posting to T Accounts, and Preparing an Adjusted Trial Balance

1. and 2.

P14. Determining Adjusting Entries, Posting to T Accounts, and Preparing an Adjusted Trial Balance (Concluded)

3.

4.

a.

b.

c.

d.

e.

f.

g.

P15. Preparing Adjusting Entries

1.

a.

b.

$$(\quad / \quad)$$
$$\times \quad =$$

c.

d.

$$+ \quad -$$
$$=$$

e.

$$[(\quad / \quad)$$
$$\times \quad]$$
$$[(\quad / \quad)$$
$$\times \quad]$$

f.

g.

$$(\quad / \quad)$$
$$\times \quad =$$

h.

2.

P16. **Determining Adjusting Entries and Tracing Their Effects to Financial Statements**

1. and 2.

3.

Note: Unearned Tax Fees does not appear on the adjusted trial balance because it now has a zero balance.

P16. Determining Adjusting Entries and Tracing Their Effects to Financial Statements (Concluded)

Assets		
Liabilities		
Owner's Equity		

4.		

CHAPTER 4—Working Papers
COMPLETING THE ACCOUNTING CYCLE

Short Exercises

SE1. Concepts Underlying Closing Entries

1.		3.	
2.		4.	

SE2. Accounting Cycle

SE3. Closing Revenue Accounts

SE4. Closing Expense Accounts

SE5. Closing the Income Summary Account

SE6. Closing the Withdrawals Account

SE7. Posting Closing Entries

SE8. Preparation of Reversing Entries

SE9. Effects of Reversing Entries

SE10. Preparation of Closing Entries

SE11. Preparation of Closing Entries from a Work Sheet

Exercises: Set A

E1A. Preparation of Closing Entries

E2A. Reversing Entries

1.

2.

3.

E3A. Preparation of a Trial Balance

E4A. Completion of a Work Sheet

1. and 2.

Account Name	Trial Balance		Adjustments		Adjusted Trial Balance		Income Statement		Balance Sheet	
	Debit	Credit	Debit	Credit	Debit	Credit	Debit	Credit	Debit	Credit

E5A. Preparation of Statement of Owner's Equity

E6A. Preparation of Adjusting and Reversing Entries from Work Sheet Columns

1.

2.

E7A. Preparation of Closing Entries from the Work Sheet

E8A. Adjusting Entries and Preparation of a Balance Sheet

1.

2.

Problems

P1. Preparation of Closing Entries

1.

2.

P2. Closing Entries Using T Accounts and Preparation of Financial Statements

1. and 2.

3.

Assets

Liabilities

Owner's Equity

4.

P3. Preparation of Closing Entries

(numbers are in thousands)

1.

2.

P4. Preparation of a Work Sheet, Financial Statements, and Adjusting, Closing, and Reversing Entries

1.

Account Name	Trial Balance		Adjustments		Adjusted Trial Balance		Income Statement		Balance Sheet	
	Debit	Credit	Debit	Credit	Debit	Credit	Debit	Credit	Debit	Credit

P4. Preparation of a Work Sheet, Financial Statements, and Adjusting, Closing, and Reversing Entries (Continued)

2.

P4. Preparation of a Work Sheet, Financial Statements, and Adjusting, Closing, and Reversing Entries (Continued)

Assets		
Liabilities		
Owner's Equity		

3.

General Journal

Date	Description	Debit	Credit
	Adjusting entries:		

P4. Preparation of a Work Sheet, Financial Statements, and Adjusting, Closing, and Reversing Entries (Concluded)

General Journal

Date		Description	Debit	Credit
		Closing entries:		
		Reversing entries:		

4.

P5. The Complete Accounting Cycle Without a Work Sheet: Two Months (*second month optional*)

1., 3., and 6.

	General Journal				Page 1
Date	**Description**	**Post. Ref.**	**Debit**		**Credit**

P5. The Complete Accounting Cycle Without a Work Sheet: Two Months (*second month optional*)
(Continued)

	General Journal			Page 2
Date	**Description**	**Post. Ref.**	**Debit**	**Credit**
	Adjusting entries:			

P5. The Complete Accounting Cycle Without a Work Sheet: Two Months (*second month optional*) (Continued)

		General Journal				Page 3
Date		Description	Post. Ref.	Debit	Credit	
		Closing entries:				

P5. **The Complete Accounting Cycle Without a Work Sheet: Two Months (*second month optional*)**
(Continued)

4.

5.

P5. The Complete Accounting Cycle Without a Work Sheet: Two Months (*second month optional*)
(Continued)

Assets		
Liabilities		
Owner's Equity		

7.

P5. The Complete Accounting Cycle Without a Work Sheet: Two Months (*second month optional*) (Continued)

8., 9., and 12.

	General Journal			Page 4
Date	**Description**	**Post. Ref.**	**Debit**	**Credit**

P5. **The Complete Accounting Cycle Without a Work Sheet: Two Months** (*second month optional*)
(Continued)

		General Journal			Page 5
Date		Description	Post. Ref.	Debit	Credit
		Adjusting entries:			
		Closing entries:			

P5. The Complete Accounting Cycle Without a Work Sheet: Two Months (*second month optional*) (Continued)

2.

Cash					Account No.		
		Post.				**Balance**	
Date	**Item**	**Ref.**	**Debit**	**Credit**	**Debit**	**Credit**	

Prepaid Insurance					Account No.		
		Post.				**Balance**	
Date	**Item**	**Ref.**	**Debit**	**Credit**	**Debit**	**Credit**	

Repair Supplies					Account No.		
		Post.				**Balance**	
Date	**Item**	**Ref.**	**Debit**	**Credit**	**Debit**	**Credit**	

4-29

P5. The Complete Accounting Cycle Without a Work Sheet: Two Months (*second month optional*)
(Continued)

Repair Equipment

Date	Item	Post. Ref.	Debit	Credit	Balance Debit	Balance Credit

Account No.

Accumulated Depreciation—Repair Equipment

Date	Item	Post. Ref.	Debit	Credit	Balance Debit	Balance Credit

Account No.

Accounts Payable

Date	Item	Post. Ref.	Debit	Credit	Balance Debit	Balance Credit

Account No.

L. Stoker, Capital

Date	Item	Post. Ref.	Debit	Credit	Balance Debit	Balance Credit

Account No.

L. Stoker, Withdrawals

Date	Item	Post. Ref.	Debit	Credit	Balance Debit	Balance Credit

Account No.

P5. The Complete Accounting Cycle Without a Work Sheet: Two Months (*second month optional*)
(Continued)

Income Summary
Account No.

Date	Item	Post. Ref.	Debit	Credit	Balance Debit	Balance Credit

Repair Revenue
Account No.

Date	Item	Post. Ref.	Debit	Credit	Balance Debit	Balance Credit

Store Rent Expense
Account No.

Date	Item	Post. Ref.	Debit	Credit	Balance Debit	Balance Credit

Advertising Expense
Account No.

Date	Item	Post. Ref.	Debit	Credit	Balance Debit	Balance Credit

P5. The Complete Accounting Cycle Without a Work Sheet: Two Months (*second month optional*) (Continued)

Insurance Expense

Account No.

Date		Item	Post. Ref.	Debit	Credit	Balance	
						Debit	Credit

Repair Supplies Expense

Account No.

Date		Item	Post. Ref.	Debit	Credit	Balance	
						Debit	Credit

Depreciation Expense—Repair Equipment

Account No.

Date		Item	Post. Ref.	Debit	Credit	Balance	
						Debit	Credit

P5. The Complete Accounting Cycle Without a Work Sheet: Two Months (*second month optional*) (Continued)

10.

P5. The Complete Accounting Cycle Without a Work Sheet: Two Months (*second month optional*)
(Continued)

11.

P5. The Complete Accounting Cycle Without a Work Sheet: Two Months (*second month optional*) (Concluded)

Assets

Liabilities

Owner's Equity

13.

P6. Preparation of Closing Entries

1.

2.

P7. Closing Entries Using T Accounts and Preparation of Financial Statements

1. and 2.

P7. Closing Entries Using T Accounts and Preparation of Financial Statements (Continued)

P7. Closing Entries Using T Accounts and Preparation of Financial Statements (Continued)

3.

P7. Closing Entries Using T Accounts and Preparation of Financial Statements (Concluded)

Assets

Liabilities

Owner's Equity

4.

P8. Preparation of Closing Entries

P9. Preparation of a Work Sheet, Financial Statements, and Adjusting, Closing, and Reversing Entries

1.

Account Name	Trial Balance		Adjustments		Adjusted Trial Balance		Income Statement		Balance Sheet	
	Debit	Credit	Debit	Credit	Debit	Credit	Debit	Credit	Debit	Credit

4-42

P9. Preparation of a Work Sheet, Financial Statements, and Adjusting, Closing, and Reversing Entries (Continued)

2.

Assets

Liabilities

Owner's Equity

P9. Preparation of a Work Sheet, Financial Statements, and Adjusting, Closing, and Reversing Entries (Continued)

3.

General Journal

Date	Description	Debit	Credit
	Adjusting entries:		

P9. Preparation of a Work Sheet, Financial Statements, and Adjusting, Closing, and Reversing Entries (Concluded)

General Journal

Date		Description	Debit	Credit
		Closing entries:		
		Reversing entry:		

4.

P10. The Complete Accounting Cycle Without a Work Sheet: Two Months (*second month optional*)

1., 3., and 6.

	General Journal			Page 1
Date	Description	Post. Ref.	Debit	Credit

P10. The Complete Accounting Cycle Without a Work Sheet: Two Months (*second month optional*) (Continued)

	General Journal				Page 2
Date	**Description**	**Post. Ref.**	**Debit**		**Credit**
	Adjusting entries:				

	General Journal			Page 3
Date	**Description**	**Post. Ref.**	**Debit**	**Credit**
	Closing entries:			

P10. The Complete Accounting Cycle Without a Work Sheet: Two Months (*second month optional*) (Continued)

4.

P10. The Complete Accounting Cycle Without a Work Sheet: Two Months (*second month optional*) (Continued)

5.

P10. The Complete Accounting Cycle Without a Work Sheet: Two Months (*second month optional*)
(Continued)

	Assets		
	Liabilities		
	Owner's Equity		

7.			

8., 9., and 12.

		General Journal			Page 4
Date		**Description**	**Post. Ref.**	**Debit**	**Credit**

		General Journal				Page 5
Date		Description	Post. Ref.	Debit	Credit	
		Adjusting entries:				
		Closing entries:				

P10. The Complete Accounting Cycle Without a Work Sheet: Two Months (*second month optional*)
(Continued)

2.

Cash   Account No. _____

Date	Item	Post. Ref.	Debit	Credit	Balance Debit	Balance Credit

Prepaid Insurance   Account No. _____

Date	Item	Post. Ref.	Debit	Credit	Balance Debit	Balance Credit

Repair Supplies   Account No. _____

Date	Item	Post. Ref.	Debit	Credit	Balance Debit	Balance Credit

P10. The Complete Accounting Cycle Without a Work Sheet: Two Months (*second month optional*) (Continued)

Repair Equipment

Account No.

Date	Item	Post. Ref.	Debit	Credit	Balance Debit	Balance Credit

Accumulated Depreciation—Repair Equipment

Account No.

Date	Item	Post. Ref.	Debit	Credit	Balance Debit	Balance Credit

Accounts Payable

Account No.

Date	Item	Post. Ref.	Debit	Credit	Balance Debit	Balance Credit

B. Lutz, Capital

Account No.

Date	Item	Post. Ref.	Debit	Credit	Balance Debit	Balance Credit

B. Lutz, Withdrawals

Account No.

Date	Item	Post. Ref.	Debit	Credit	Balance Debit	Balance Credit

P10. The Complete Accounting Cycle Without a Work Sheet: Two Months (*second month optional*)
(Continued)

Income Summary   Account No.

Date	Item	Post. Ref.	Debit	Credit	Balance Debit	Balance Credit

Repair Revenue   Account No.

Date	Item	Post. Ref.	Debit	Credit	Balance Debit	Balance Credit

Store Rent Expense   Account No.

Date	Item	Post. Ref.	Debit	Credit	Balance Debit	Balance Credit

Advertising Expense   Account No.

Date	Item	Post. Ref.	Debit	Credit	Balance Debit	Balance Credit

Insurance Expense   Account No.

Date		Item	Post. Ref.	Debit	Credit	Balance Debit	Balance Credit

Repair Supplies Expense   Account No.

Date		Item	Post. Ref.	Debit	Credit	Balance Debit	Balance Credit

Depreciation Expense—Repair Equipment   Account No.

Date		Item	Post. Ref.	Debit	Credit	Balance Debit	Balance Credit

P10. The Complete Accounting Cycle Without a Work Sheet: Two Months (*second month optional*) (Continued)

10.

Assets

Liabilities

Owner's Equity

13.

FOUNDATIONS OF FINANCIAL REPORTING AND THE CLASSIFIED BALANCE SHEET

Short Exercises

SE1. Objectives and Qualitative Characteristics

a.	
b.	
c.	
d.	
e.	

SE2. Enhancing Qualitative Characteristics and Accounting Conventions

1.	
2.	
3.	
4.	
5.	
6.	
7.	

SE3. Classification of Accounts: Balance Sheet

1.	
2.	
3.	
4.	
5.	
6.	
7.	
8.	
9.	

SE4. Classified Balance Sheet

Assets

Liabilities

Owner's Equity

SE5. Liquidity Ratios

Current Assets	=		+		+		+	
	=							

Working Capital	=	Current Assets	–	Current Liabilities
	=		–	

Current Ratio	=	$\dfrac{\text{Current Assets}}{\text{Current Liabilities}}$	=		=	

SE6. Profitability Ratios

1.	Profit Margin	=	$\dfrac{\text{Net Income}}{\text{Net Sales}}$	=		=	
2.	Asset Turnover	=	$\dfrac{\text{Net Sales}}{\text{Average Total Assets}}$	=		=	times
3.	Return on Assets	=	$\dfrac{\text{Net Income}}{\text{Average Total Assets}}$	=		=	
4.	Debt to Equity Ratio	=	$\dfrac{\text{Total Liabilities}}{\text{Total Owner's Equity}}$	=		=	
5.	Return on Equity	=	$\dfrac{\text{Net Income}}{\text{Average Total Owner's Equity}}$	=		=	

SE7. Profitability Ratios

Profit Margin	×	Asset Turnover		=	Return on Assets	
	×		times	=		

Return on Assets	/		Return on Equity	
	/			

Exercises: Set A

E1A. Financial Accounting Concepts

1.		12.	
2.		13.	
3.		14.	
4.		15.	
5.		16.	
6.		17.	
7.		18.	
8.		19.	
9.		20.	
10.		21.	
11.		22.	

E2A. Qualitative Characteristics and Accounting Conventions

1.	
2.	
3.	
4.	
5.	
6.	
7.	
8.	
9.	
10.	
11.	

E3A. Classification of Accounts: Balance Sheet

1.		9.	
2.		10.	
3.		11.	
4.		12.	
5.		13.	
6.		14.	
7.		15.	
8.		16.	

E4A. Classified Balance Sheet Preparation

Assets

Liabilities

Owner's Equity

E5A. Liquidity Ratios

1.

2. Current Ratio $= \dfrac{\text{Current Assets}}{\text{Current Liabilities}} = \underline{\hspace{2cm}} = $

E6A. Profitability Ratios

1. Profit Margin $=\dfrac{\text{Net Income}}{\text{Net Sales}}$

$$=\dfrac{\rule{2cm}{0.4pt}}{\rule{2cm}{0.4pt}}=$$

2. Asset Turnover $=\dfrac{\text{Net Sales}}{\text{Average Total Assets}}$

$$=\dfrac{\rule{3cm}{0.4pt}}{(\rule{2cm}{0.4pt}+\rule{2cm}{0.4pt})\ /}$$

$$=\dfrac{\rule{2cm}{0.4pt}}{\rule{2cm}{0.4pt}}=\quad\text{times}$$

3. Return on Assets $=\dfrac{\text{Net Income}}{\text{Average Total Assets}}$

$$=\dfrac{\rule{2cm}{0.4pt}}{\rule{2cm}{0.4pt}}=$$

4. Debt to Equity Ratio $=\dfrac{\text{Total Liabilities}}{\text{Total Owner's Equity}}$

$$=\dfrac{\rule{2cm}{0.4pt}}{\rule{2cm}{0.4pt}}=$$

5. Return on Equity $=\dfrac{\text{Net Income}}{\text{Average Owner's Equity}}$

$$=\dfrac{\rule{3cm}{0.4pt}}{(\rule{2cm}{0.4pt}+\rule{2cm}{0.4pt})\ /\ }$$

$$=\dfrac{\rule{2cm}{0.4pt}}{\rule{2cm}{0.4pt}}=$$

E7A. Liquidity and Profitability Ratios

1.

a.

Current Assets	
Current Liabilities	
Working Capital	

b. Current Ratio $= \dfrac{\text{Current Assets}}{\text{Current Liabilities}} = \underline{\qquad} = \underline{\qquad}$

2.

a. Profit Margin $= \dfrac{\text{Net Income}}{\text{Net Sales}} = \underline{\qquad} = \underline{\qquad}$

b. Asset Turnover $= \dfrac{\text{Net Sales}}{\text{Average Total Assets}}$

$= \dfrac{}{(\underline{\qquad} + \underline{\qquad})\ /}$

$= \underline{\qquad} = \underline{\qquad}$ times

c. Return on Assets $= \dfrac{\text{Net Income}}{\text{Average Total Assets}} = \underline{\qquad} = \underline{\qquad}$

d. Debt to Equity Ratio $= \dfrac{\text{Total Liabilities}}{\text{Total Owner's Equity}} = \underline{\qquad} = \underline{\qquad}$

e. Return on Equity $= \dfrac{\text{Net Income}}{\text{Average Owner's Equity}}$

$= \dfrac{}{(\underline{\qquad} + \underline{\qquad})\ /}$

$= \underline{\qquad} =$

E8A. Liquidity and Profitability Ratios

1.(a)

	Current Assets	Current Liabilities	Working Capital	Current Ratio	

1.(b)

	Net Income	Sales	Profit Margin	Average Total Asset	Assets Turnover	Return on Assets	Average Owner's Equity	Return on Equity

E8A. Liquidity and Profitability Ratios (Concluded)

2.

	Total Liabilities	Owner's Equity	Debt to Equity Ratio	

Problems

P1. Qualitative Characteristics and Accounting Conventions

1.

2.

3.

4.

5.

6.

7.

8.

P2. Classified Balance Sheet

1.

Assets

Liabilities

Owner's Equity

P2. Classified Balance Sheet (Concluded)

2.	a.	Current Ratio	=	$\dfrac{\text{Current Assets}}{\text{Current Liabilities}}$	
			=	======= =	
	b.	Debt to Equity Ratio	=	$\dfrac{\text{Total Liabilities}}{\text{Owner's Equity}}$	
			=	======= =	

3.

P3. Liquidity and Profitability Ratios

1. **a.** **Working Capital**

	2014	2013	

b. $$\text{Current Ratio} = \frac{\text{Current Assets}}{\text{Current Liabilities}}$$

2014: ———————— =

2013: ———————— =

2. **a.** $$\text{Profit Margin} = \frac{\text{Net Income}}{\text{Net Sales}}$$

2014: ———————— =

2013: ———————— =

P3. Liquidity and Profitability Ratios (Continued)

b. Asset Turnover $= \dfrac{\text{Net Sales}}{\text{Average Total Assets}}$

2014: (_____ + _____) /

= _____ = _____ times

2013: (_____ + _____) /

= _____ = _____ times

c. Return on Assets $= \dfrac{\text{Net Income}}{\text{Average Total Assets}}$

2014: (_____ + _____) /

= _____ =

2013: (_____ + _____) /

= _____ =

d. Debt to Equity Ratio $= \dfrac{\text{Total Liabilities}}{\text{Owner's Equity}}$

2014: _____ =

2013: _____ =

P3. Liquidity and Profitability Ratios (Concluded)

e.	Return on Equity	=	$\dfrac{\text{Net Income}}{\text{Average Owner's Equity}}$

2014:

(_____ + _____) / _____

= _____ = _____

2013:

(_____ + _____) / _____

= _____ = _____

1.

Assets

Liabilities

Owner's Equity

P4. Classified Balance Sheet (Concluded)

2.	a.	Current Ratio	=	Current Assets / Current Liabilities	
			=	____ =	
	b.	Debt to Equity Ratio	=	Total Liabilities / Owner's Equity	
			=	____ =	

3.

Alternate Problems

P5. Accounting Conventions

1.

2.

3.

4.

5.

6.

7.

8.

P6. Classified Balance Sheet

1.

Assets

Liabilities

Owner's Equity

P6. Classified Balance Sheet (Concluded)

2.	a.	Current Ratio	=	$\dfrac{\text{Current Assets}}{\text{Current Liabilities}}$	
		2014	————	=	
	b.	Debt to Equity Ratio	=	$\dfrac{\text{Total Liabilities}}{\text{Total Owner's Equity}}$	
		2014	————	=	

3.

P7. Liquidity and Profitability Ratios

1. **a.** **Working Capital**

	2014	2013	

b. **Current Ratio** = $\dfrac{\text{Current Assets}}{\text{Current Liabilities}}$

2014: ⎯⎯⎯⎯⎯⎯ =

2013: ⎯⎯⎯⎯⎯⎯ =

2. **a.** **Profit Margin** = $\dfrac{\text{Net Income}}{\text{Net Sales}}$

2014: ⎯⎯⎯⎯⎯⎯ =

2013: ⎯⎯⎯⎯⎯⎯ =

P7. Liquidity and Profitability Ratios (Continued)

b.

$$\text{Asset Turnover} = \frac{\text{Net Sales}}{\text{Average Total Assets}}$$

2014:

$$= (\qquad + \qquad) / \qquad$$

$$= \frac{\qquad}{\qquad} = \qquad \text{times}$$

2013:

$$= (\qquad + \qquad) / \qquad$$

$$= \frac{\qquad}{\qquad} = \qquad \text{times}$$

c.

$$\text{Return on Assets} = \frac{\text{Net Income}}{\text{Average Total Assets}}$$

2014:

$$= (\qquad + \qquad) / \qquad$$

$$= \frac{\qquad}{\qquad} = \qquad$$

2013:

$$= (\qquad + \qquad) / \qquad$$

$$= \frac{\qquad}{\qquad} = \qquad$$

d.

$$\text{Debt to Equity Ratio} = \frac{\text{Total Liabilities}}{\text{Owner's Equity}}$$

2014:

$$\frac{\qquad}{\qquad} = \qquad$$

2013:

$$\frac{\qquad}{\qquad} = \qquad$$

P7. Liquidity and Profitability Ratios (Concluded)

e.		Return on Equity	=	$\dfrac{\text{Net Income}}{\text{Average Owner's Equity}}$	

2014:

$($ _____ + _____ $) /$

$=$ _____ $=$

2013:

$($ _____ + _____ $) /$

$=$ _____ $=$

P8. Classified Balance Sheet

1.

Assets

Liabilities

Owner's Equity

P8. Classified Balance Sheet (Concluded)

2.

a.

$$\text{Current Ratio} = \frac{\text{Current Assets}}{\text{Current Liabilities}}$$

2014 ————— =

b.

$$\text{Debt to Equity Ratio} = \frac{\text{Total Liabilities}}{\text{Total Owner's Equity}}$$

2014 ————— =

3.

CHAPTER 6—Working Papers

ACCOUNTING FOR MERCHANDISING OPERATIONS

Short Exercises

SE1. Characteristics of Inventory Systems

1.	
2.	
3.	
4.	
5.	
6.	
7.	

SE2. Single-Step Income Statement

SE3. Multistep Income Statement

SE4. Terms of Sale

(×)	

SE5. Sales and Sales Returns

		−		=	
		×		=	
		−		=	

SE6. Purchases of Merchandise: Perpetual Inventory System

SE7. Purchases of Merchandise: Periodic Inventory System

SE8. Cost of Goods Sold: Periodic Inventory System

SE9. Sales of Merchandise: Periodic Inventory System

SE10. Operating Cycle

SE11. Identification of Management Issues

1.	
2.	
3.	
4.	

Exercises: Set A

E1A. Concept Identification

1.		3.	
2.		4.	

E2A. Classification of Accounts: Income Statement

1.		7.	
2.		8.	
3.		9.	
4.		10.	
5.		11.	
6.		12.	

E3A. Preparation of Income Statements

1.

2.

E4A. Multistep Income Statement

E5A. Terms of Sale

E6A. Purchases Involving Discounts: Perpetual Inventory System

			−		=				
			×		=				
			−		=				
		+		=					

E7A. Sales Involving Discounts: Periodic Inventory System

				−	=	
				×	=	
				−	=	
		+		=		

E8A. Preparation of the Income Statement: Perpetual Inventory System

E9A. Recording Purchases: Perpetual Inventory System

E10A. Recording Sales: Perpetual Inventory System

E11A. Preparation of the Income Statement: Periodic Inventory System

E12A. Merchandising Income Statement: Missing Data, Multiple Years

(in thousands)

	2014	2013	2012

E13A. Recording Purchases: Periodic Inventory System

E14A. Recording Sales: Periodic Inventory System

E15A. Foreign Merchandising Transactions

		×		=	
		×		=	
		−		=	

Problems

P1. Forms of the Income Statement

1.

	2014	%*	2013	%*

*Rounded

2.

P2. Merchandising Income Statement: Perpetual Inventory System

1.

2.

P3. Merchandising Transactions: Perpetual Inventory System

1.

P3. Merchandising Transactions: Perpetual Inventory System (Concluded)

2.

P4. Merchandising Income Statement: Periodic Inventory System

1.

P4. Merchandising Income Statement: Periodic Inventory System (Concluded)

2.

P5. Merchandising Transactions: Periodic Inventory System

1.

P5. Merchandising Transactions: Periodic Inventory System (Concluded)

2.

1.

2.

Alternate Problems

P7. Forms of the Income Statement

1.

	2014	%*	2013	%*

*Rounded

2.

P8. Merchandising Income Statement: Perpetual Inventory System

1.

P8. Merchandising Income Statement: Perpetual Inventory System (Concluded)

2.

P9. Merchandising Transactions: Perpetual Inventory System

1.

P9. Merchandising Transactions: Perpetual Inventory System (Concluded)

2.

P10. Merchandising Transactions: Periodic Inventory System

1.

2.

P11. Merchandising Income Statement: Periodic Inventory System

1.

2.

P12. Merchandising Transactions: Periodic Inventory System

1.

SPECIAL-PURPOSE JOURNALS

Problems

P1. Cash Receipt and Cash Payments Journals

1. and 2.

			Debits			Credits		
							Cash Receipts Journal	Page 1
Date	Account Debited/Credited	Post. Ref.	Cash	Sales Discounts	Other Accounts	Accounts Receivable	Sales	Other Accounts

P1. Cash Receipt and Cash Payments Journals (Concluded)

Cash Payments Journal Page 1

Date	Ck. No.	Payee	Account Credited/Debited	Post. Ref.	Cash	Credits		Debits			
						Purchases Discounts	Other Accounts	Accounts Payable	Salaries Expense	Rent Expense	Other Accounts

3.

P2. Purchases and General Journals

1.

		General Journal			Page 1
Date		**Description**	**Post. Ref.**	**Debit**	**Credit**

P2. **Purchases and General Journals** (Continued)

2.

Purchases Journal

Page 1

Date	Account Credited	Date of Invoice	Terms	Post. Ref.	Credit	Debits				Other Accounts		
					Accounts Payable	Purchases	Freight In	Store Supplies	Office Supplies	Account	Post. Ref.	Amount

3.

General Ledger

Store Supplies   Account No.

Date	Item	Post. Ref.	Debit	Credit	Balance Debit	Balance Credit

Office Supplies   Account No.

Date	Item	Post. Ref.	Debit	Credit	Balance Debit	Balance Credit

Lawn Equipment   Account No.

Date	Item	Post. Ref.	Debit	Credit	Balance Debit	Balance Credit

Display Equipment   Account No.

Date	Item	Post. Ref.	Debit	Credit	Balance Debit	Balance Credit

Cleaning Equipment   Account No.

Date	Item	Post. Ref.	Debit	Credit	Balance Debit	Balance Credit

Accounts Payable   Account No.

Date	Item	Post. Ref.	Debit	Credit	Balance Debit	Balance Credit

P2. Purchases and General Journals (Concluded)

Purchases

Account No.

Date	Item	Post. Ref.	Debit	Credit	Balance Debit	Balance Credit

Purchases Returns and Allowances

Account No.

Date	Item	Post. Ref.	Debit	Credit	Balance Debit	Balance Credit

Freight In

Account No.

Date	Item	Post. Ref.	Debit	Credit	Balance Debit	Balance Credit

Accounts Payable Subsidiary Ledger

Brandon Lawn Equipment Company

Date	Item	Post. Ref.	Debit	Credit	Balance

Diego Fertilizer Company

Date	Item	Post. Ref.	Debit	Credit	Balance

Laronne Supply, Inc.

Date	Item	Post. Ref.	Debit	Credit	Balance

Whitman Company

Date	Item	Post. Ref.	Debit	Credit	Balance

P3. Comprehensive Use of Special-Purpose Journals

1., 5., and 6.

	Sales Journal					Page 1
Date	Account Debited	Invoice Number	Terms	Post. Ref.	Debit Accounts Receivable/ Credit Sales	

6S-7

P3. Comprehensive Use of Special-Purpose Journals (Continued)

Purchases Journal

Page 1

Date	Account Credited	Date of Invoice	Terms	Credit — Accounts Payable (Post. Ref.)	Credit — Accounts Payable	Debits — Purchases	Debits — Freight In	Debits — Other Accounts — Account	Debits — Other Accounts — Post. Ref.	Debits — Other Accounts — Amount

Cash Receipts Journal

Page 1

Date	Account Debited/Credited	Post. Ref.	Debits — Cash	Debits — Sales Discounts	Debits — Other Accounts	Credits — Accounts Receivable	Credits — Sales	Credits — Other Accounts

6S-8

P3. Comprehensive Use of Special-Purpose Journals (Continued)

Page 1

Cash Payments Journal

Date	Ck. No.	Payee	Account Credited/Debited	Post. Ref.	Credits				Debits			
					Cash	Purchases Discounts	Other Accounts	Accounts Payable	Salaries Expense	Advertising Expense	Rent Expense	Other Accounts

6S-9

P3. Comprehensive Use of Special-Purpose Journals (Continued)

	General Journal			Page 1
Date	**Description**	**Post. Ref.**	**Debit**	**Credit**

2., 5., and 6.

General Ledger

Cash   Account No.

		Post.			Balance	
Date	**Item**	**Ref.**	**Debit**	**Credit**	**Debit**	**Credit**

Accounts Receivable   Account No.

		Post.			Balance	
Date	**Item**	**Ref.**	**Debit**	**Credit**	**Debit**	**Credit**

Store Equipment   Account No.

		Post.			Balance	
Date	**Item**	**Ref.**	**Debit**	**Credit**	**Debit**	**Credit**

Accounts Payable   Account No.

		Post.			Balance	
Date	**Item**	**Ref.**	**Debit**	**Credit**	**Debit**	**Credit**

Notes Payable — Account No. _____

| | | Post. | | | Balance | |
Date	Item	Ref.	Debit	Credit	Debit	Credit

Linda Berrill, Capital — Account No. _____

| | | Post. | | | Balance | |
Date	Item	Ref.	Debit	Credit	Debit	Credit

Sales — Account No. _____

| | | Post. | | | Balance | |
Date	Item	Ref.	Debit	Credit	Debit	Credit

Sales Discounts — Account No. _____

| | | Post. | | | Balance | |
Date	Item	Ref.	Debit	Credit	Debit	Credit

Sales Returns and Allowances — Account No. _____

| | | Post. | | | Balance | |
Date	Item	Ref.	Debit	Credit	Debit	Credit

Purchases — Account No. _____

| | | Post. | | | Balance | |
Date	Item	Ref.	Debit	Credit	Debit	Credit

Purchases Discounts — Account No. _____

| | | Post. | | | Balance | |
Date	Item	Ref.	Debit	Credit	Debit	Credit

Purchases Returns and Allowances — Account No. _____

| | | Post. | | | Balance | |
Date	Item	Ref.	Debit	Credit	Debit	Credit

P3. Comprehensive Use of Special-Purpose Journals (Continued)

Freight In — Account No.

Date	Item	Post. Ref.	Debit	Credit	Balance Debit	Balance Credit

Salaries Expense — Account No.

Date	Item	Post. Ref.	Debit	Credit	Balance Debit	Balance Credit

Advertising Expense — Account No.

Date	Item	Post. Ref.	Debit	Credit	Balance Debit	Balance Credit

Rent Expense — Account No.

Date	Item	Post. Ref.	Debit	Credit	Balance Debit	Balance Credit

3. and 5.

Accounts Receivable Subsidiary Ledger

Midtown Center

Date	Item	Post. Ref.	Debit	Credit	Balance

Steve Oahani

Date	Item	Post. Ref.	Debit	Credit	Balance

Missy Porter

Date	Item	Post. Ref.	Debit	Credit	Balance

P3. Comprehensive Use of Special-Purpose Journals (Continued)

4. and 5.

Accounts Payable Subsidiary Ledger

Chassman Books, Inc.

Date	Item	Post. Ref.	Debit	Credit	Balance

Lakeside Books

Date	Item	Post. Ref.	Debit	Credit	Balance

Menden Shippers

Date	Item	Post. Ref.	Debit	Credit	Balance

Perspectives Publishing Company

Date	Item	Post. Ref.	Debit	Credit	Balance

7.

INVENTORIES

Short Exercises

SE1. Inventory Concepts

1.		3.		5.	
2.		4.		6.	

SE2. Specific Identification Method

			(		×	)		
			(		×	)		

SE3. Average-Cost Method: Periodic Inventory System

		×	=		

SE4. FIFO Method: Periodic Inventory System

			(		×	)		
			(		×	)		

SE5. LIFO Method: Periodic Inventory System

			(		×	)		
			(		×	)		

SE6. Effects of Inventory Costing Methods and Changing Prices

	Specific Identification Method	Periodic Inventory System		
		Average-Cost Method	FIFO Method	LIFO Method

SE7. Average-Cost Method: Perpetual Inventory System

			Units	Cost per Unit	Amount*
	(		+	)	

*Rounded

SE8. FIFO Method: Perpetual Inventory System

			Units	Cost per Unit		
	(	+	)			

SE9. LIFO Method: Perpetual Inventory System

			Units	Cost per Unit		
	(	+	)			

SE10. Retail Inventory Method

	Cost	Retail
=		

	=	
	=	
	=	
	=	

SE11. Management Issues

1.	3.	5.
2.	4.	

SE12. Inventory Turnover and Days' Inventory on Hand

Inventory Turnover	=	Cost of Goods Sold / Average Inventory	
	=	+ /	
	=	= times	
Days' Inventory on Hand	=	Number of Days in a Year / Average Inventory	
	=	= days	

Exercises: Set A

E1A. Accounting Conventions and Inventory Valuation

E2A. Periodic Inventory System and Inventory Costing Methods

1. Specific identification method

		−		=	

2. Average-cost method

		/		=	

		×		

3. FIFO method

E2A. Periodic Inventory System and Inventory Costing Methods (Concluded)

4. LIFO method

5.

E3A. Periodic Inventory System and Inventory Costing Methods

1. FIFO method

	Year 1	Year 2	Year 3

2. LIFO method

	Year 1	Year 2	Year 3

3.

E4A. Periodic Inventory System and Inventory Costing Methods

1.

			×		
			×		
			×		
			×		
			×		

(×)

| × | = | |
| × | = | |

| × | = | |
| × | = | |

2.

E5A. Effects of Inventory Costing Methods on Cash Flows

1.

				FIFO Method	LIFO Method
		×			
		×			
		×			
		×			
	(	×	)		
	(	×	)		

E5A. Effects of Inventory Costing Methods on Cash Flows (Concluded)

2.

				FIFO Method	LIFO Method
		×			
		×			
		×			
		×			
		×			
	(	×	)		
	(	×	)		

E6A. Perpetual Inventory System and Inventory Costing Methods

1. Average-cost method

Date			Units	Cost	Amount

FIFO method

Date			Units	Cost	Amount

E6A. Perpetual Inventory System and Inventory Costing Methods (Concluded)

LIFO method

Date			Units	Cost	Amount

2.

E7A. Periodic and Perpetual Systems and Inventory Costing Methods

Cost of goods available for sale and ending inventory in units

	Units	Cost	Total

1. Periodic inventory system

a. Specific identification method:

		×		=			
		×		=			
		×		=			

b. Average-cost method:

c.   FIFO method:

				×		=	
				×		=	

d.   LIFO method:

				×		=	
				×		=	
				×		=	

2.   Perpetual inventory system

a.

	Units	Cost	Amount

E7A. Periodic and Perpetual Systems and Inventory Costing Methods (Concluded)

b. **FIFO method:**

					×		
					×		
					×		
					×		

	=		−		=		

c. **LIFO method:**

					×		
					×		
					×		

	=		−		=		

E8A. Retail Method

1.		Cost	Retail
	=		

2.			

E9A. Gross Profit Method

E10A. Management Issues

1.		5.	
2.		6.	
3.		7.	
4.			

E11A. Inventory Ratios

Inventory Turnover	=	$\dfrac{\text{Cost of Goods Sold}}{\text{Average Inventory}}$	
2013	=	$\dfrac{}{(+) / }$	
	=	$\dfrac{}{} = $	times
2014	=	$\dfrac{}{(+) / }$	
	=	$\dfrac{}{} = $	times
Days' Inventory on Hand	=	$\dfrac{\text{Number of Days in a Year}}{\text{Inventory Turnover}}$	
2013	=	$\dfrac{\text{days}}{\text{times}} = $	days
2014	=	$\dfrac{\text{days}}{\text{times}} = $	days

E12A. Effects of Inventory Errors

	2014	2013

Problems

P1. Periodic Inventory System and Inventory Costing Methods

1.

	Units	Price	Total Cost

2.   **a.**   Average-cost method:

	×			

	/	
(　　　　 – 　　　　)	×	

P1. Periodic Inventory System and Inventory Costing Methods (Continued)

b. FIFO method:

c. LIFO method:

P1. Periodic Inventory System and Inventory Costing Methods (Concluded)

3.

	Average-Cost			FIFO			LIFO		
(	+	)	/	(	+	)	/	(	+	)	/
(		times	)	(		times	)	(		times	)
(	/		)	(	/		)	(	/		)
(	days		times	)	(	days		times	)	(	days		times	)
	days	/			days	/			days	/	

P2. Periodic Inventory System and Inventory Costing Methods

1. Periodic inventory system—average-cost method

	Units	Unit Price	Amount

	Units	Unit Price	Amount			

2. Periodic inventory system—FIFO method

	Units	Unit Price	Amount

P2. Periodic Inventory System and Inventory Costing Methods (Continued)

					Units	Unit Price	Amount
		Units	Unit Price	Amount			
(	×	)					
(	×	)					

3. Periodic inventory system—LIFO method

	Units	Unit Price	Amount

(	×	)	
(	×	)	

				Unit	
			Units	Price	Amount
		Unit				
	Units	Price	Amount			

4.

P3. Perpetual Inventory System and Inventory Costing Methods

1. Perpetual inventory system—average-cost method

Date			Units	Cost	Amount

P3. Perpetual Inventory System and Inventory Costing Methods (Continued)

2. Perpetual inventory system—FIFO method

Date			Units	Cost	Amount

P3. Perpetual Inventory System and Inventory Costing Methods (Continued)

3. **Perpetual inventory system—LIFO method**

Date			Units	Cost	Amount

4.

P4. Retail Method

1.							Cost	Retail
				———— =				
			×	=				

2.								
			×	=				

3.								

4.								

P5. Gross Profit Method

1.

2.

Alternate Problems

P6. Periodic Inventory System and Inventory Costing Methods

1.

	Units	Price	Total Cost

2. **a.** **Average-cost method:**

(		×	)		

P6. Periodic Inventory System and Inventory Costing Methods (Continued)

b. FIFO method:

c. LIFO method:

P6. Periodic Inventory System and Inventory Costing Methods (Concluded)

3.	Average-Cost			FIFO			LIFO		
	(	+	) /	(	+	) /	(	+	) /
	(	/	)	(	/	)	(	/	)
	times			times			times		
	days			days			days		
	(days /	times	)	(days /	times	)	(days /	times	)

P7. Periodic Inventory System and Inventory Costing Methods

1. Periodic inventory system—average-cost method

	Units	Unit Price	Amount

	Units	Unit Price	Amount			

P7. Periodic Inventory System and Inventory Costing Methods (Continued)

2. Periodic inventory system—FIFO method

	Units	Unit Price	Amount

	Units	Unit Price	Amount			

3. Periodic inventory system—LIFO method

	Units	Unit Price	Amount

	Units	Unit Price	Amount			

4.

P8. Perpetual Inventory System and Inventory Costing Methods

1. Perpetual inventory system—average-cost method

Date			Units	Cost	Amount

2. Perpetual inventory system—FIFO method

Date			Units	Cost	Amount

P8. Perpetual Inventory System and Inventory Costing Methods (Concluded)

3. Perpetual inventory system—LIFO method

Date			Units	Cost	Amount

4.

P9. Retail Method

1. Month-end inventory at cost estimated

	Cost	Retail
Ratio of cost to retail price: ———— =		
× =		
2. × =		
3.		
4.		

P10. Gross Profit Method

1.

2.

CASH AND INTERNAL CONTROL

Short Exercises

SE1. Internal Control

1.	
2.	
3.	
4.	

SE2. Components of Internal Control

1.		4.	
2.		5.	
3.			

SE3. Limitations of Internal Control

1.		3.	
2.		4.	

SE4. Separation of Duties

1.	
2.	
3.	

SE5. Physical Controls

1.		4.	
2.		5.	
3.			

SE6. Internal Control Activities

1.		5.	
2.		6.	
3.		7.	
4.			

SE7. Business Documents

SE8. Cash and Cash Equivalents

SE9. Bank Reconciliation

SE10. Petty Cash Fund

E1A. Components of Internal Control

1.		6.	
2.		7.	
3.		8.	
4.		9.	
5.			

E2A. Control Procedures

1.	
2.	
3.	
4.	

E3A. Internal Control Procedures

1.	
2.	
3.	
4.	
5.	

E4A. Business Documents

	Prepared by	Received by	
1.			
2.			
3.			
4.			
5.			
6.			
7.			

E5A. Use of Accounting Records in Internal Control (Answers may vary)

1.

2.

3.

4.

E6A. Cash and Cash Equivalents

E7A. Bank Reconciliation

E8A. Imprest System

E9A. Petty Cash Transactions

a.						
b.						
c.						

E10A. Management and Auditor Responsibility for Internal Control

Problems

P1. Internal Control Components

1.	1.		6.	
	2.		7.	
	3.		8.	
	4.		9.	
	5.			

2.	

	P2. Internal Control Procedures
1.	*Authorization*
	Recording transactions
	Documents and records
	Physical controls
	Periodic independent verification
	Separation of duties
	Sound personnel practices
2.	

P2. Internal Control Procedures

8-8

P3. Internal Control Activities

1.

a. *Authorization*

b. *Recording transactions*

c. *Documents and records*

d. *Physical controls*

e. *Periodic independent verification*

f. *Separation of duties*

g. *Sound personnel practices*

2.

P4. Bank Reconciliation

1.

2.

3.

P4. Bank Reconciliation (Concluded)

4.

P5. Imprest (Petty Cash) Transaction

1.

2.

Alternative Problems

P6. Internal Control Components

1.	1.		6.	
	2.		7.	
	3.		8.	
	4.		9.	
	5.			

2.	

P7. Control Activities

1.	1.		6.	
	2.		7.	
	3.		8.	
	4.		9.	
	5.			

2.	a.	*Authorization*
	b.	*Recording transactions*
	c.	*Documents and records*
	d.	*Physical controls*
	e.	*Periodic independent verification*
	f.	*Separation of duties*

P7. Control Activities

8-14

P7. Control Activities (Concluded)

	g.	***Sound personnel practices***

P8. Internal Control Activities

1.   *Cash sales*

Purchases

2.

P9. Bank Reconciliation

1.

2.

3.

P9. Bank Reconciliation (Concluded)

4.

P10. Imprest (Petty Cash) Fund Transactions

1.

2.

CHAPTER 9—Working Papers

RECEIVABLES

Short Exercises

SE1. Accounts Receivable and Notes Receivable

1.	
2.	
3.	
4.	
5.	

SE2. Evaluating the Level of Accounts Receivable

SE3. Percentage of Net Sales Method

SE4. Accounts Receivable Aging Method

a.

b.

SE5. Write-off of Accounts Receivable

	Before Write-off	After Write-off

SE6. Interest Computations*

a.		×		/		×		/		=	
b.		×		/		×		/		=	
c.		×		/		×		/		=	
d.		×		/		×		/		=	
e.		×		/		×		/		=	

*Rounded

SE7. Notes Receivable Calculations

		Principal	×	Rate of Interest	×	Time	=	Interest*
			×	/	×	/	=	

*Rounded

		Principal	+	Interest	=	Maturity Value
			+		=	

SE8. Notes Receivable Calculations

		Principal	×	Rate of Interest	×	Time	=	Interest*
			×	/	×	/	=	

*Rounded

		Principal	+	Interest	=	Maturity Value
			+		=	

SE9. Management Issues

1.	
2.	
3.	
4.	

SE10. Short-Term Liquidity Ratios

a.	Receivables Turnover	=	$\dfrac{\text{Net Sales}}{\text{Average Accounts Receivable}}$	
		=	(_____ + _____) / _____	
		=	_____ = _____ times	
b.	Days' Sales Uncollected	=	$\dfrac{\text{365 days}}{\text{Receivables Turnover}}$	
		=	$\dfrac{\text{days}}{\text{_____}}$ = _____ days*	

*Rounded

Exercises: Set A

E1A. Evaluating the Level of Accounts Receivable

E2A. Percentage of Net Sales Method

E3A. Accounts Receivable Aging Method

a.

b.

E4A. Aging Method and Net Sales Method Contrasted

Accounts Receivable

Allowance for Uncollectible Accounts

a.

Allowance for Uncollectible Accounts

b.

Allowance for Uncollectible Accounts

E5A. Aging Method and Net Sales Method Contrasted

Percentage of net sales method:

Accounts receivable aging method:

E6A. Aging Method and Net Sales Method Contrasted

a. | **Percentage of net sales method:**

b. | **Accounts receivable aging method:**

E7A. Write-off of Accounts Receivable

Accounts Receivable

Allowance for Uncollectible Accounts

	Before Write-off	After Write-off

E8A. Interest Computations*

a.		×		/		×		/	=
b.		×		/		×		/	=
c.		×		/		×		/	=
d.		×		/		×		/	=
e.		×		/		×		/	=

*Rounded

E9A. Notes Receivable Calculations

Principal	×	Rate of Interest	×	Time	=	Interest*
	×	/	×	/	=	

*Rounded

Principal	+	Interest	=	Maturity Value
	+		=	

E10A. Notes Receivable Calculations

Principal	×	Rate of Interest	×	Time	=	Interest*
	×	/	×	/	=	

Principal	×	Rate of Interest	×	Time	=	Interest*
	×	/	×	/	=	

Principal	+	Interest	=	Maturity Value
	+		=	

*Rounded

E11A. Notes Receivable Calculations

a.

Principal	×	Rate of Interest	×	Time	=	Interest*
	×	/	×	/	=	

*Rounded

Principal	+	Interest	=	Maturity Value
	+		=	

b.

Principal	×	Rate of Interest	×	Time	=	Interest*
	×	/	×	/	=	

*Rounded

Principal	+	Interest	=	Maturity Value
	+		=	

E12A. Management Issues

1.	
2.	
3.	
4.	
5.	
6.	
7.	
8.	
9.	

E13A. Short-Term Liquidity Ratios

$$\text{Receivables Turnover} = \frac{\text{Net Sales}}{\text{Average Accounts Receivable}}$$

$$= \frac{}{(+) / }$$

$$= \frac{}{} = \text{ times*}$$

$$\text{Days' Sales Uncollected} = \frac{365 \text{ days}}{\text{Receivables Turnover}}$$

$$= \frac{ \text{days}}{ \text{times}} = \text{days*}$$

*Rounded

Problems

P1. Methods of Estimating Uncollectible Accounts and Receivables Analysis

1.

2.

a. Percentage of net sales method:

Uncollectible Accounts Expense	=	Net Credit Sales	×	2.5 percent
	=	(	−	) ×
	=			

Allowance for Uncollectible Accounts	=		−	
	=			

Accounts Receivable, Net	=		−	
	=			

b. Accounts receivable aging method:

Uncollectible Accounts Expense	=		+	
	=			

Allowance for Uncollectible Accounts	=			

Accounts Receivable, Net	=		−	
	=			

P1. Methods of Estimating Uncollectible Accounts and Receivables Analysis (Concluded)

3.

Receivables Turnover = $\dfrac{\underline{\hspace{3cm}} - \underline{\hspace{2cm}}}{(\underline{\hspace{2cm}} + \underline{\hspace{2cm}}) \, / \, \underline{\hspace{2cm}}}$

$= \dfrac{\underline{\hspace{3cm}}}{\underline{\hspace{1cm}}} = \underline{\hspace{2cm}}$ times*

Days' Sales Uncollected $= \dfrac{\text{days}}{\underline{\hspace{3cm}}} = \underline{\hspace{2cm}}$ days*

*Rounded

4.

P2. Accounts Receivable Aging Method

1.

Customer Account	Total	Not Yet Due	1–30 Days Past Due	31–60 Days Past Due	61–90 Days Past Due	Over 90 Days Past Due

2.

3.

	Amount	Percentage Considered Uncollectible	Allowance for Uncollectible Accounts*

*Rounded

4.

5.

P3. Notes Receivable Calculations

1.

Principal	×	Rate of Interest	×	Time	=	Interest*	
	×	/	×	/	=		

*Rounded

Principal	+	Interest	=	Maturity Value	
	+		=		

Principal	×	Rate of Interest	×	Time	=	Interest*	
	×	/	×	/	=		

*Rounded

Principal	+	Interest	=	Maturity Value	
	+		=		

P3. Notes Receivable Calculations (Concluded)

Principal	×	Rate of Interest	×	Time	=	Interest*
	×	/	×	/	=	

*Rounded

Principal	+	Interest	=	Maturity Value
	+		=	

2.

Date of Note		Principal	×	Rate of Interest	×	Time	=	Interest*
			×	/	×	/	=	
			×	/	×	/	=	
			×	/	×	/	=	

*Rounded

3.

P4. Notes Receivable Calculations

1.

2.

Principal	×	Rate of Interest	×	Time	=	Interest*
	×	/	×	/	=	

*Rounded

3.

Principal	+	Rate of Interest	=	Maturity Value
	+		=	

4.

Principal	×	Rate of Interest	×	Time	=	Interest*
	×	/	×	/	=	

*Rounded

5.

Principal	×	Rate of Interest	×	Time	=	Interest
	×	/	×	/	=	

or:

	−		=	

6.

Alternate Problems

P5. Methods of Estimating Uncollectible Accounts and Receivables Analysis

1.

2.

a. Percentage of net sales method:

Uncollectible Accounts Expense	=	Net Credit Sales	×	1.6 percent
	=	(−) ×		
	=			

Allowance for Uncollectible Accounts	=		+	
	=			

Accounts Receivable, Net	=		−	
	=			

b. Accounts receivable aging method:

Uncollectible Accounts Expense	=		−	
	=			

Allowance for Uncollectible Accounts	=			

Accounts Receivable, Net	=		−	
	=			

3.

Receivables Turnover = $\dfrac{\rule{4cm}{0.4pt} - \rule{2cm}{0.4pt}}{(\rule{2cm}{0.4pt} + \rule{2cm}{0.4pt})\ /\ \rule{1cm}{0.4pt}}$

$= \dfrac{\rule{3cm}{0.4pt}}{} = \rule{2cm}{0.4pt}$ times*

Days' Sales Uncollected = $\dfrac{\text{days}}{\rule{3cm}{0.4pt}} = \rule{2cm}{0.4pt}$ days*

*Rounded

4.

P6. Accounts Receivable Aging Method

1.

Customer Account	Total	Not Yet Due	1–30 Days Past Due	31–60 Days Past Due	61–90 Days Past Due	Over 90 Days Past Due

2.

P6. Accounts Receivable Aging Method (Concluded)

3.

	Amount	Percentage Considered Uncollectible	Allowance for Uncollectible Accounts*

*Rounded

4.

5.

P7. Notes Receivable Calculations

1.

Principal	×	Rate of Interest	×	Time	=	Interest*
	×	/	×	/	=	

*Rounded

Principal	+	Interest	=	Maturity Value
	+		=	

Principal	×	Rate of Interest	×	Time	=	Interest*
	×	/	×	/	=	

*Rounded

Principal	+	Interest	=	Maturity Value
	+		=	

P7. Notes Receivable Calculations (Concluded)

	Principal	×	Rate of Interest	×	Time	=	Interest*	
		×	/	×	/	=		

*Rounded

	Principal	+	Interest	=	Maturity Value	
		+		=		

2.

Date of Note	Principal	×	Rate of Interest	×	Time	=	Interest*	
		×	/	×	/	=		
		×	/	×	/	=		
		×	/	×	/	=		

*Rounded

3.

P8. Notes Receivable Calculations

1.

2.

Principal	×	Rate of Interest	×	Time	=	Interest*
	×	/	×	/	=	

3.

Principal	+	Interest	=	Maturity Value
	+		=	

4.

Principal	×	Rate of Interest	×	Time	=	Interest*
	×	/	×	/	=	

5.

Principal	×	Rate of Interest	×	Time	=	Interest*
	×	/	×	/	=	

or:

	−		=	

6.

*Differences in calculations due to rounding.

LONG-TERM ASSETS

SE1. Classifying Cost of Long-Term Assets

1.		5.	
2.		6.	
3.		7.	
4.		8.	

SE2. Group Purchase

Asset	Appraisal	Percentage	Apportionment*	

*			

SE3. Straight-Line Method

Depreciation for each year:

(		–		) /		=

SE4. Production Method

Depreciation for

Year 1:	(		–		) ×	————	=	
Year 2:	(		–		) ×	————	=	
Year 3:	(		–		) ×	————	=	
Year 4:	(		–		) ×	————	=	

SE5. Double-Declining-Balance Method

Depreciation for

Year 1:			×		=	
Year 2:	(	−	) ×		=	
Year 3:	(	−	) ×		=	
Year 4:		−			=	

SE6. Disposal of Plant Assets: No Trade-In

1.

Carrying Value	=	Equipment	−	Accumulated Depreciation—Equipment
	=		−	
	=			

2.

a.

Gain (Loss) on Disposal of Equipment	=	Cash Received	−	Carrying Value
	=		−	
	=			

b.

Gain (Loss) on Sale of Equipment	=	Cash Received	−	Carrying Value
	=		−	
	=			

c.

Gain (Loss) on Sale of Equipment	=	Cash Received	−	Carrying Value
	=		−	
	=			

SE7. Natural Resources

Depletion charge per ton:

(		–		) /		tons	=		per ton

Depletion expense for the first year:

	tons ×		=	

Depreciation expense for the first year:

	×		tons /		tons)	=	

SE8. Intangible Assets: Computer Software

SE9. Management Issues

1.		4.	
2.		5.	
3.		6.	

SE10. Free Cash Flow

Free Cash Flow	=	Net Cash Flows from Operating Activities	–	Dividends	–	Purchases of Plant Assets	+	Sales of Plant Assets
	=		–		–		+	

Exercises: Set A

E1A. Recognition and Classification of Capital Expenditures

1.	
2.	
3.	
4.	
5.	
6.	

E2A. Recognizing and Classifying the Cost of Long-Term Assets

E3A. Group Purchase

Asset	Appraisal	Percentage	Apportionment*	

*			

E4A. Cost of Long-Term Asset and Depreciation

	/		=	

E5A. Depreciation Methods

1.	Depreciation computed by straight-line method:

	/		=	

2.	Depreciation computed by production method:

	×		/		=	

3.	Depreciation computed by double-declining-balance method:

		×		=	
		×	(	–	)
=		×		=	

Adjusting entry:

Balance sheet presentation:

E6A. Double-Declining-Balance Method

Year 1		×			=								
Year 2		×	(		−		)	=		×		=	
Year 3		×	(		−		)	=		×		=	
Year 4		−				=			−		=		

E7A. Revision of Depreciation Rates

First-year depreciation:

	/		=	

Second-year depreciation:

	/		=	
Depreciation to date:				

Remaining depreciable cost:

	−		=	

Remaining useful life:

	years	−		years	=		years

Third-year depreciation:

	/		=	

E8A. Disposal of Plant Assets

Carrying Value	=	Equipment	–	Accumulated Depreciation—Equipment
	=		–	
	=			

1.

Gain (Loss) on Disposal of Equipment	=	Cash Received	–	Carrying Value
	=		–	
	=			

2.

Gain (Loss) on Sale of Equipment	=	Cash Received	–	Carrying Value
	=		–	
	=			

3.

Gain (Loss) on Sale of Equipment	=	Cash Received	–	Carrying Value
	=		–	
	=			

E9A. Disposal of Plant Assets

			(		–		) /	years		
			×		/		=			
1.										
				years	×		=			
2.										
3.										

E10A. Natural Resource Depletion and Depreciation of Related Plant Assets

Depletion charge per ton:

(		–		)	/		tons	=		per ton

Depletion expense for the first year:

	tons	×		=	

E11A. Amortization of Copyrights and Trademarks

1.

2.

E12A. Accounting for a Patent

a.

b.

c.

| | / | years | = | |

d.

	− (	×	)	
=			

E13A. Management Issues

1.		5.	
2.		6.	
3.		7.	
4.			

E14A. Free Cash Flow

Free Cash Flow	=	Net Cash Flows from Operating Activities	−	Dividends	−	Purchases of Plant Assets	+	Sale of Plant Assets
	=		−		−		+	

Problems

P1. Identification of Long-Term Assets Terminology

1.

1.	6.
2.	7.
3.	8.
4.	9.
5.	10.

2.

P2. Determining Cost of Assets

1.

	Land	Land Improvements	Building	Equipment

2.

P3. Comparison of Depreciation Methods

1.

				Depreciation Table		
	Depreciation Method	Year	Computation		Depreciation	Carrying Value
a.	Straight-line		/			
			/			
			/			
			/			
b.	Production		× ————			
			× ————			
			× ————			
			× ————			
c.	Double-declining-balance		×			
			×			
			×			
			−			

2.

a.			(	−	)	
b.			(	−	)	
c.			(	−	)	

3.

P4. Comparison of Depreciation Methods

1.

			Depreciation Table			
		Depreciation Method	Year	Computation	Depreciation	Carrying Value
a.	Straight-line			/		
				/		
				/		
				/		
				/		
				/		
b.	Production			× ———		
				× ———		
				× ———		
				× ———		
				× ———		
				× ———		
c.	Double-declining-balance			×		
				×		
				×		
				×		
				−		

2.

a.	A gain of		(	−		)
b.	A gain of		(	−		)
c.	A gain of		(	−		)

3.

P5. Natural Resource Depletion and Depreciation of Related Plant Assets

1.

	÷	

2.

	×	

3.

(	/	)		×	

4.

		×	
a.			
b.			
(	/	)	

5.

Alternate Problems

P6. Determining Cost of Assets

1.

	Land	Land Improvements	Buildings	Machinery	Expense

2.

P7. Comparison of Depreciation Methods

1.

	Depreciation Method	Year	Computation		Depreciation	Carrying Value
a.	**Straight-line**		/			
			/			
			/			
			/			
b.	**Production**		×—————			
			×—————			
			×—————			
			×—————			
c.	**Double-declining-balance**		×			
			×			
			×			
			–			

2.

a.			(	–	)	
b.			(	–	)	
c.			(	–	)	

3.

P8. Comparison of Depreciation Methods

1.

<table>
<tr><th colspan="6">Depreciation Table</th></tr>
<tr><th colspan="2">Depreciation
Method</th><th>Year</th><th colspan="2">Computation</th><th>Depreciation</th><th>Carrying
Value</th></tr>
<tr><td>a.</td><td>Straight-line</td><td></td><td>/</td><td></td><td></td><td></td></tr>
<tr><td></td><td></td><td></td><td>/</td><td></td><td></td><td></td></tr>
<tr><td></td><td></td><td></td><td>/</td><td></td><td></td><td></td></tr>
<tr><td></td><td></td><td></td><td>/</td><td></td><td></td><td></td></tr>
<tr><td></td><td></td><td></td><td>/</td><td></td><td></td><td></td></tr>
<tr><td></td><td></td><td></td><td>/</td><td></td><td></td><td></td></tr>
<tr><td>b.</td><td>Production</td><td></td><td>×</td><td></td><td></td><td></td></tr>
<tr><td></td><td></td><td></td><td>×</td><td></td><td></td><td></td></tr>
<tr><td></td><td></td><td></td><td>×</td><td></td><td></td><td></td></tr>
<tr><td></td><td></td><td></td><td>×</td><td></td><td></td><td></td></tr>
<tr><td></td><td></td><td></td><td>×</td><td></td><td></td><td></td></tr>
<tr><td></td><td></td><td></td><td>×</td><td></td><td></td><td></td></tr>
<tr><td>c.</td><td>Double-
declining-
balance</td><td></td><td>×</td><td></td><td></td><td></td></tr>
<tr><td></td><td></td><td></td><td>×</td><td></td><td></td><td></td></tr>
<tr><td></td><td></td><td></td><td>×</td><td></td><td></td><td></td></tr>
<tr><td></td><td></td><td></td><td>×</td><td></td><td></td><td></td></tr>
<tr><td></td><td></td><td></td><td>−</td><td></td><td></td><td></td></tr>
</table>

2.

a.		(	−	)	
b.		(	−	)	
c.		(	−	)	

3.

P9. Natural Resource Depletion and Depreciation of Related Plant Assets

1.

	÷	

2.

	×	

3.

(	/	)		×	

4.

			×	
a.				
b.				
(	/	)		

5.

CURRENT LIABILITIES AND
FAIR VALUE ACCOUNTING

Short Exercises

SE1. Issues in Accounting for Liabilities

1.		3.		5.	
2.		4.			

SE2. Interest Expense on Note Payable

1.

2.

$\times$ / $\times$

/ =

SE3. Payroll Expenses

1.

2.

/ =

− =

$\times$ =

$\times$ =

SE4. Product Warranty Liability

			(		×	)	

SE5. Types of Liabilities

1.		4.		7.	
2.		5.			
3.		6.			

SE6. Simple and Compound Interest

1.	**Simple interest**				
		×	/	=	

2.	**Compounded semiannually**				
		×	/	=	
		×	/	=	

3.	**Compounded quarterly at 3% for 4 periods**				
		×	/	=	
		×	/	=	
		×	/	=	
		×	/	=	

SE7. Present Value Calculations

1.

		×		=	

2.

		×		=	

3.

		×		=	

4.

		×		=	

SE8. Valuing an Asset for the Purpose of Making a Purchasing Decision

SE9. Measuring Short-Term Liquidity

Working Capital	=	Current Assets – Current Liabilities
	=	– =

Payables Turnover	=	Cost of Goods Sold +/– Change in Merchandise Inventory
		Average Accounts Payable
	=	+
		(+) /
	=	= times

Days' Payable	=	365 days	=	=	days
		Payables Turnover			

Exercises: Set A

E1A. Issues in Accounting for Liabilities

1.		4.		7.	
2.		5.		8.	
3.		6.			

E2A. Interest Expense on Note Payable

1.

2.

$\times$ / $\times$ /

=

3.

$\times$ / $\times$ /

=

E3A. Sales and Excise Taxes

1.

/ =

2.

$\times$ / =

$\times$ / =

E4A. Payroll Expenses

1.

2.

			/		=	
			−		=	
			×		=	
			×		=	

E5A. Product Warranty Liability

1.

2.

(×)

E6A. Vacation Pay Liability

1.

(		−		)	×		×		=	

2. and 3.

E7A. Contingencies and Commitments

1.

2.

E8A. Determining an Advance Payment

E9A. Present Value Calculations

1.

		×		=	

2.

		×		=	

3.

		×		=	

4.

		×		=	

E10A. Present Value of a Lump-Sum Contract

	Years	Rate	Factor from Table 1*				Present Value of $30,000
1.				×		=	
2.				×		=	
3.				×		=	
4.				×		=	

*Table 1 in Appendix B

E11A. Present Value of an Annuity Contract

	Payments	Rate	Factor from Table 2*				Present Value of $2,400 Payments
1.				×		=	
2.				×		=	
3.				×		=	
4.				×		=	

*Table 2 in Appendix B

E12A. Valuing an Asset for the Purpose of Making a Purchasing Decision

E13A. Deferred Payment

	Future Payment	×	Factor (3 periods, 4%)	=	Present Value	
		×		=		

E14A. Negotiating the Sale of a Business

Knight offer to sell:

From Table 2 in Appendix B:

	Periodic Cash Flow	×	Factor (20 periods, 12%)	=	Present Value	
		×		=		

Bosh's offer to buy:

From Table 2 in Appendix B:

	Periodic Cash Flow	×	Factor (10 periods, 12%)	=	Present Value	
		×		=		

E15A. Measuring Short-Term Liquidity

2013

Working Capital	=	**Current Assets – Current Liabilities**				
	=		–		=	

Payables Turnover	=	**Cost of Goods Sold +/– Change in Merchandise Inventory**
		Average Accounts Payable

	=		+			
		(	+	) /		

	=		=	**times***

Days' Payable	=	**365 days**	=		=	**days***
		Payables Turnover				

*Rounded

2014

Working Capital	=	**Current Assets – Current Liabilities**				
	=		–		=	

Payables Turnover	=	**Cost of Goods Sold +/– Change in Merchandise Inventory**
		Average Accounts Payable

	=		–			
		(	+	) /		

	=		=	**times***

Days' Payable	=	**365 days**	=		=	**days**
		Payables Turnover				

*Rounded

Problems

P1. Identification of Current Liabilities, Contingencies, and Commitments

1.	1.		8.	
	2.		9.	
	3.		10.	
	4.		11.	
	5.		12.	
	6.		13.	
	7.		14.	

2.	

P2. Notes Payable and Wages Payable

Part A

1.

									×		×		/				
									=								

									×		×		/				
									=								

2.

P2. Notes Payable and Wages Payable (Concluded)

Part B

1.

2.

			/	=		
			−	=		
			×	=		
			×	=		

P3. Product Warranty Liability

1.

a.

				×		=			

b.

				×		×		=		

2.

3.

P4. Identification and Evaluation of Current Liabilities

1.

	(	×	)	
	(	×	)	
	(	×	)	
	(	×	)	
	(	×	)	
	(	×	)	
	(	×	)	

2.

3.

Working Capital	=	Current Assets − Current Liabilities
	=	− =

$$\text{Payables Turnover} = \frac{\text{Cost of Goods Sold } +/- \text{ Change in Merchandise Inventory}}{\text{Average Accounts Payable}}$$

	=	+ +	=	=	times*

$$\text{Days' Payable} = \frac{365 \text{ days}}{\text{Payables Turnover}} = \frac{\text{days}}{\text{times}} = \text{days*}$$

*Rounded

P5. Applications of Present Value

1.	a.					
			×		=	
	b.					
			×		=	

2.	

P6. Identification of Current Liabilities, Contingencies, and Commitments

1.

1.		8.		
2.		9.		
3.		10.		
4.		11.		
5.		12.		
6.		13.		
7.		14.		

2.

P7. Notes Payable and Wages Payable

Part A

1.

					×		×	/	
			=						
					×		×	/	
			=						

2.

P7. Notes Payable and Wages Payable (Concluded)

Part B

1.

2.

			/		=			
			−		=			
			×		=			
			×		=			

P8. Product Warranty Liability

1.

a.

b.

				×	×	=

2.

3.

P9. Identification and Evaluation of Current Liabilities

1.

	(		×	)	
	(		×	)	
	(		×	)	
	(		×	)	
	(		×	)	
	(		×	)	
	(		×	)	

2.

3.

Working Capital	=	Current Assets − Current Liabilities
	=	− =

Payables Turnover	=	$\dfrac{\text{Cost of Goods Sold } +/-\text{ Change in Merchandise Inventory}}{\text{Average Accounts Payable}}$
	=	+ + = = times*

| Days' Payable | = | $\dfrac{365 \text{ days}}{\text{Payables Turnover}}$ = $\dfrac{\text{days}}{\text{times}}$ = days* |

*Rounded

P10. Applications of Present Value

1. **a.**

	×		=	

b.

	×		=	

2.

CHAPTER 12—Working Papers

ACCOUNTING FOR PARTNERSHIPS

Short Exercises

SE1. Partnership Characteristics

1.		4.	
2.		5.	
3.			

SE2. Partnership Formation

SE3. Distribution of Partnership Income

Computation of capital ratios:

Division of income:

SE4. Distribution of Partnership Income

	Income of Partner		Income
	Martin	**Steven**	**Distributed**

SE5. Distribution of Partnership Income

	Income (Loss) of Partner		Income
	Martin	Steven	Distributed

SE6. Withdrawal of a Partner

SE7. Admission of a New Partner

SE8. Admission of a New Partner

SE9. Withdrawal of a Partner

SE10. Liquidation of a Partnership

SE11. Types of Partnerships

1.		4.	
2.		5.	
3.			

Exercises: Set A

E1A. Partnership Characteristics

1.	
2.	
3.	
4.	
5.	

E2A. Partnership Advantages and Disadvantages

1.	
2.	
3.	
4.	

E3A. Partnership Formation

E4A. Distribution of Income

1. Computation: **The partners share equally.**

Note: Because the partnership agreement does not address the distribution of income and losses, the law requires that income and losses be shared equally.

2. Computation: **The partners agreed to share the income three-fifths to Shah and two-fifths to Ruben.**

3. Computation: **The partners agreed to share the income in the ratio of their original investments.**

4. Computation:

	Income of Partner		Income
	Shah	Ruben	Distributed

E5A. Distribution of Income or Losses: Salaries and Interest

1. Computation:

			Income (Loss) of Partner		Income Distributed
			Shah	Ruben	

2. Computation:

			Income (Loss) of Partner		Income Distributed
			Shah	Ruben	

E5A. Distribution of Income or Losses: Salaries and Interest (Concluded)

3.	Computation:		Income (Loss) of Partner		Loss Distributed
			Shah	Ruben	

4.	Computation:		Income (Loss) of Partner		Loss Distributed
			Shah	Ruben	

E6A. Distribution of Income: Average Capital Balance

Average capital balances computed:

Partner	Date	Capital Balance	×	Months Unchanged	=	Total		Average Capital

Average capital balance ratios computed:

Distribution of income computed:

E7A. Admission of a New Partner: Recording a Bonus

1.

Computation:

*****Distribution of bonus from original partners:**

2.

Computation:

*****Distribution of bonus to original partners:**

E8A. Withdrawal of a Partner

Computation:

*Distribution of bonus from remaining partners:

E9A. Partnership Liquidation

1.

2.

E10A. Partnership Liquidation

12-15

Problems

P1. Partnership Formation and Distribution of Income

1.

2.

a. Income shared equally

				2013	2014

b.

c. Income shared on the basis of the partners' original investments.

					2013	2014

P1. Partnership Formation and Distribution of Income (Continued)

d. Interest on investments; remainder shared equally.

2013 computation:						Income of Partner		Income
						Thomas	Lopez	Distributed

2014 computation:						Income of Partner		Income
						Thomas	Lopez	Distributed

P1. Partnership Formation and Distribution of Income (Continued)

e. **Salaries allowed; remainder shared equally.**

2013 computation:	Income of Partner		Income
	Thomas	Lopez	Distributed

2014 computation:	Income of Partner		Income
	Thomas	Lopez	Distributed

P1. Partnership Formation and Distribution of Income (Concluded)

f. Interest and salaries allowed; remainder shared equally.

2013 computation:			Income of Partner		Income Distributed
			Thomas	Lopez	

2014 computation:			Income of Partner		Income Distributed
			Thomas	Lopez	

3.

P2. Distribution of Income: Salaries and Interest

1.

	Income of Partner		Income
	Wilkes	Chevron	Distributed

2.

	Income of Partner		Income
	Wilkes	Chevron	Distributed

3.

	Income (Loss) of Partner		Loss
	Wilkes	Chevron	Distributed

P3. Admission and Withdrawal of a Partner

1. a.

b.

c.

Computation:

*Distribution of bonus to original partners:

Partners' capital ratios:

Partner	Capital Balance	Ratios	

P3. Admission and Withdrawal of a Partner (Concluded)

d.

Computation:

***Distribution of bonus from original partners:**

Partners' capital ratios: See answer to part c.

e.

***Distribution of bonus from original partners:**

f.

2.

P4. Partnership Liquidation

1.

Explanation	Cash	Other Assets	Accounts Payable	Josh, Capital (40%)	John, Capital (40%)	Hassan, Capital (20%)	Gain (or Loss) from Realization
a. Sale of Other Assets							
b. Payment of Liabilities							
c. Distribution of Gain (or Loss) from Realization							
d. Distribution of Cash to Partners							

12-23

P4. Partnership Liquidation (Concluded)

2.

a.

b.

c.

d.

Alternate Problems

P5. Distribution of Income: Salaries and Interest

1.

	Income of Partner			Income
	Jan	Pat	Misa	Distributed

2.

	Income of Partner			Income
	Jan	Pat	Misa	Distributed

P5. Distribution of Income: Salaries and Interest (Concluded)

3.

					Income (Loss) of Partner			Income
					Jan	Pat	Misa	Distributed

P6. Admission and Withdrawal of a Partner

1.

a.

b.

c.

Computation:

*Distribution of bonus to original partners:

d.

P6. Admission and Withdrawal of a Partner (Concluded)

Computation:

*Distribution of bonus from original partners to Rob:

e.

*Distribution between the remaining partners of excess cash over Sasha's capital balance:

f.

2.

P7. Partnership Liquidation

1.

Explanation	Cash	Accounts Receivable	Inventory	Equipment (net)	Accounts Payable	Gauri, Capital (50%)	Tailor, Capital (30%)	Pavel, Capital (20%)	Gain (or Loss) from Realization
a. Sale of Accounts Receivable									
b. Sale of Inventory									
c. Sale of Equipment									
d. Payment of Accounts Payable									
e. Distribution of Gain (or Loss) from Realization									
f. Distribution of Partners' Share of Gauri's Deficit*									
g. Distribution of Cash to Tailor and Pavel									

12-29

P7. Partnership Liquidation (Concluded)

2.

a.

b.

c.

d.

e.

f.

g.

P8. Comprehensive Partnership Transactions

Computation:		Income of Partner		Income
		Zadoney	Slater	Distributed

P8. Comprehensive Partnership Transactions (Continued)

Computation:

***Distribution of bonus from original partners:**

P8. Comprehensive Partnership Transactions (Continued)

Computation:				Income (Loss) of Partner			Income
				Zadoney	Slater	Nissan	Distributed
		*					
		**					

*	Zadoney:	
**	Slater:	

P8. Comprehensive Partnership Transactions (Continued)

P8. Comprehensive Partnership Transactions (Concluded)

Zadoney, Slater, and Nissan Partnership
Statement of Liquidation
January 1, 2015

Explanation	Cash	Accounts Receivable (net)	Land	Building (net)	Equipment (net)	Accounts Payable	Mortgage Payable	Zadoney, Capital (33.33%)	Slater, Capital (33.33%)	Nissan, Capital (33.33%)	Gain (or Loss) from Realization
									**	***	

* Zadoney
** Slater
*** Nissan

12-35

CHAPTER 13—Working Papers
ACCOUNTING FOR CORPORATIONS

Short Exercises

SE1. Advantages and Disadvantages of a Corporation

1.		4.	
2.		5.	
3.		6.	

SE2. Effect of Start-up and Organization Costs

SE3. Management Issues

1.		5.	
2.		6.	
3.			
4.			

SE4. Stockholders' Equity

SE5. Preferred Stock Dividends with Dividends in Arrears

	Preferred Stock Dividends		Common Stock Dividends		Total Dividends
	Amount	Per Share	Amount	Per Share	Allocated
2013	—	—	—	—	—
2014					
(×)					
(×)					
(−)					
2015					
(×)					
(−)					

SE6. Issuance of Stock

1.			

2.			

SE7. Issuance of Stock for Noncash Assets

1.

=		

2.

SE8. Treasury Stock Transactions

		(×)			
		(×)			
		(×)			
		(×)			
		(×)			

SE9. Retirement of Treasury Stock

SE10. Cash Dividends

Note: No entry necessary for June 1.

SE11. Stock Dividends

			(	×	)		
		×		=			

SE12. Stock Split

After Stock Split	

SE13. Effects of Stockholders' Equity Actions

	Total Assets	Total Liabilities	Total Stockholders' Equity	
1.				
2.				
3.				
4.				

SE14. Statement of Stockholders' Equity

1.		(	/	)	
2.		(	/	)	
3.		(	/	)	
4.		(	/	)	

SE15. Book Value for Preferred and Common Stock

Preferred Stock Book Value per Share	=	(		×		)	+		
					shares				

	=		=		per share

Common Stock Book Value per Share	=			−			
				shares			

	=		=		per share

SE16. Dividend Yield and Price/Earnings Ratio

Dividend Yield	=	Dividends per Share
		Market Price per Share

	=		=	

Price/Earnings (P/E) Ratio	=	Market Price per Share
		Earnings per Share

	=		=		times

Exercises: Set A

E1A. Advantages and Disadvantages of a Corporation

1.		4.	
2.		5.	
3.			

E2A. Stockholders' Equity

E3A. Characteristics of Common and Preferred Stock

1.		4.		7.	
2.		5.		8.	
3.		6.		9.	

13-9

E4A. Cash Dividends with Dividends in Arrears

					Preferred Stock Dividends		Common Stock Dividends		Total Dividends Allocated
					Amount	Per Share	Amount	Per Share	
2011					—	—	—	—	—
2012									
	(		×	)					
	(		−	)					
2013									
	(		−	)					
	(		×	)					
	(		−	)					
2014									
	(		×	)					
	(		−	)					

E5A. Cash Dividends on Preferred and Common Stock

		Preferred Stock Dividends	Common Stock Dividends	Total
1.				
	(×)			
	(−)			
2.				
	(×)			
	(−)			
	(−)			
	(×)			
	(−)			

E6A. Stock Entries Using T Accounts; Stockholders' Equity

1.

2.

Stockholders' Equity

E7A. Issuance of Stock

1.

2.

3.

4.

E8A. Issuance of Stock for Noncash Assets

1.

2.

3.

E9A. Treasury Stock Transactions

E10A. Treasury Stock Transactions Including Retirement

E11A. Cash Dividends

Note: No entry necessary for June 15.

E12A. Cash Dividends

Note: No entry necessary for November 1.

E13A. Journal Entries: Stock Dividends

(×)

×

=

E14A. Stock Split

Before Stock Split

After Stock Split

E15A. Stock Split

Before Stock Split

After Stock Split

E16A. Statement of Stockholders' Equity

	$100 Par Value, 9% Cumulative Preferred Stock	$2 Par Value Common Stock	Additional Paid-in Capital	Retained Earnings	Treasury Stock	Total
a.						
b.						
c.						
d.						
e.						
f.						

13-18

E17A. Book Value for Preferred and Common Stock

Preferred Stock **Book Value per Share**	=	(		×		)	+	
					shares			
	=				=		per share	

Common Stock **Book Value per Share**	=			− (		
					shares	
	=				=	per share*

*Rounded

E18A. Dividend Yield and Price/Earnings Ratio

Dividend Yield	=	Dividends per Share	
		Market Price per Share	
	=		=

Price/Earnings (P/E) Ratio	=	Market Price per Share	
		Earnings per Share	
	=		=	times

Problems

P1. Common Stock Transactions and Stockholders' Equity

1.

2.

3.

P2. Preferred and Common Stock Dividends and Dividend Yield

1.

	Cumulative Preferred Stock Dividends		Common Stock Dividends		
	Amount	Per Share*	Amount	Per Share**	Total Dividends Allocated

2.

	Noncumulative Preferred Stock Dividends		Common Stock Dividends		
	Amount	Per Share*	Amount	Per Share**	Total Dividends Allocated
2011					
2012					
2013					
2014					

3.

Dividend Yield $=$ $\dfrac{\text{Dividends per Share}}{\text{Market Price per Share}}$

2013 $=$ $\dfrac{}{}$ $=$

2014 $=$ $\dfrac{}{}$ $=$

* Amount of dividend / 5,000 shares

** Amount of dividend / 100,000 shares

13-21

P2. Preferred and Common Stock Dividends and Dividend Yield (Concluded)

4.

P3. Comprehensive Stockholders' Equity Transactions

1.

			Debited		Credited	
			Account Number	Dollar Amount	Account Number	Dollar Amount

Common Shares			
	shares		
	×		=

2.

P4. Comprehensive Stockholders' Equity Transactions and Stockholders' Equity

1.

					×		×	/	=	
							×		=	

2.

3.

Dividend Yield	=	$\dfrac{\text{Dividends per Share}}{\text{Market Price per Share}}$
	=	$\underline{\hspace{3cm}}$ =

Price/Earnings (P/E) Ratio	=	$\dfrac{\text{Market Price per Share}}{\text{Earnings per Share}}$
	=	$\underline{\hspace{3cm}}$ = **times**

Return on Equity	=	$\dfrac{\text{Net Income}}{\text{Average Stockholders' Equity}}$
	=	(+) /
	=	$\underline{\hspace{3cm}}$ =

4.

P5. Treasury Stock

1.

Note: There are abnormal balances because there are no data about the beginning balances and some accounting entries have decreased the account balances.

2.

P6. Dividends, Stock Splits, and Stockholders' Equity

1.

+	=	
×	=	

2.

3.

P7. Comprehensive Stockholders' Equity Transactions

1.

T accounts for stockholders' equity

2.

3.

		/		shares =		per share	

(		–		) / (		shares +		shares)
=		/	—	shares =		per share		

Alternate Problems

P8. Common Stock Transactions and Stockholders' Equity

1.

2.

3.

P9. Preferred and Common Stock Dividends and Dividend Yield

1.

	Cumulative Preferred Stock Dividends		Common Stock Dividends		Total Dividends Allocated
	Amount	Per Share*	Amount	Per Share**	

2.

	Noncumulative Preferred Stock Dividends		Common Stock Dividends		Total Dividends Allocated
	Amount	Per Share*	Amount	Per Share**	

3.

$$\text{Dividends Yield} = \frac{\text{Dividends per Share}}{\text{Market Price per Share}}$$

$$\frac{\quad\quad}{\quad\quad} = \quad\quad$$

$$\frac{\quad\quad}{\quad\quad} = \quad\quad$$

*	Amount of dividend / 40,000 shares
**	Amount of dividend / 600,000 shares

P9. Preferred and Common Stock Dividends and Dividend Yield (Concluded)

4.	

P10. Comprehensive Stockholders' Equity Transactions and Financial Ratios

1.

Note: No entry necessary for October 25.

2.

Stockholders' Equity		

3.

$$\text{Dividend Yield} = \frac{\text{Dividends per Share}}{\text{Market Price per Share}}$$

$$= \frac{}{} = $$

$$\text{Price/Earnings (P/E) Ratio} = \frac{\text{Market Price per Share}}{\text{Earnings per Share}}$$

$$= \frac{}{} = \text{times*}$$

$$\text{Return on Equity} = \frac{\text{Net Income}}{\text{Average Stockholders' Equity}}$$

$$= \frac{}{(+) \, / \,}$$

$$= \frac{}{} = *$$

* Rounded

4.

13-36

P11. Comprehensive Stockholders' Equity Transactions

1.

			Debited		Credited	
			Account Number	Dollar Amount	Account Number	Dollar Amount

	Common Shares		
		shares	
	×		=

2.

P12. Treasury Stock

1.

Note: There are abnormal balances because there are no data about the beginning balances and some accounting entries have decreased the account balances.

2.

1.

	+		=	
	×	=		

2.

P13. Dividends, Stock Splits, and Stockholders' Equity (Concluded)

3.

P14. Comprehensive Stockholders' Equity Transactions

1.

P14. Comprehensive Stockholders' Equity Transactions (Continued)

T accounts for stockholders' equity

*Cash dividends declared and stock dividends declared reduce Retained Earnings.

P14. Comprehensive Stockholders' Equity Transactions (Concluded)

2.

3.

| | / | shares | = | per share* |

(–) / (shares + shares)
= / = per share

* **Rounded**

LONG-TERM LIABILITIES

Short Exercises

SE1. Types of Long-Term Liabilities

1.		5.	
2.		6.	
3.		7.	
4.			

SE2. Mortgage Payable

Month	Monthly Payment	Interest for 1 Month at 0.6667% on Unpaid Balance	Reduction in Debt	Unpaid Balance at End of Period	
		*			
		*			
		*			

* Rounded

SE3. Bond Characteristics

1.		4.	
2.		5.	
3.		6.	

SE4. Valuing Bonds Using Present Value

Choice A

	×			
	×			

Choice B

	×			
	×			

SE5. Straight-Line Method

				×		=							
			/	(		years	×	)					
		=											
				×		×		/					
		=											
			/	(		years	×	)					
		=											
				×		×		/					
		=											
		(		×		×		/	)				
		−(		×		×		/	)				
		=		−			=						

SE7. Year-End Accrual of Bond Interest

		(		×		×		/		) –			
		(		×		×		/		)			
		=		–			=						
			×		×		/						
		=											

SE8. Bond Retirement

			×		=				
			×		=				

SE9. Bond Conversion

				×		=				
					×		=			
			_____	×		=				
				=		+				
		=								

SE10. Bond Issue Between Interest Dates

1.

			×		×	/	=			
			×		×	/	=			

2.

SE11. Leases and Pensions Definitions

1.		4.	
2.		5.	
3.			

SE12. Bond Versus Common Stock Financing

1.		4.	
2.		5.	
3.			

Exercises: Set A

E1A. Mortgage Payable

1.

Month	Monthly Payment	Interest for 1 Month at 1% on Unpaid Balance	Reduction in Debt	Unpaid Balance at End of Period

2.

E2A. Bond Issue Features and Bond Characteristics

1.		6.	
2.		7.	
3.		8.	
4.		9.	
5.			

E3A. Valuing Bonds Using Present Value

Choice A

	×			
	×			

Choice B

	×			
	×			

E4A. Valuing Bonds Using Present Value

a.

		×		
		×		

b.

		×		
		×		

c.

		×		
		×		

d.

		×		
		×		

e.

		×		
		×		

E5A. Zero Coupon Bonds

Face value of 30-year, 10% zero coupon bonds, compounded annually:

		=	
			/

Face value of 50-year, 10% zero coupon bonds, compounded annually:

		=	
			/

Face value of 30-year, 8% zero coupon bonds, compounded annually:

		=	
			/

Face value of 50-year, 8% zero coupon bonds, compounded annually:

		=	
			/

E5A. Zero Coupon Bonds

E6A. Straight-Line Method

1.

a.

			×		=	

b.

c.

2.

a.

		×		×		/		=	

b.

(		/	years	)	/		=	

c.

		−		=	

3.

a.

		×		×		/		=	

b.

(		/	years	)	/		=	

c.

		−		=	

Note: Part 2 and Part 3 are identical.

E7A. Straight-Line Method

				/	(	years	×	)			
		=									
			×	(		/	)				
		=									
			+		=						
				/	(	years	×	)			
		=									
			×	(		/	)				
		=									
			+		=						

E8A. Effective Interest Method

1. | **a.**
| | | × | | = | |

b. | |

c. | |

2. | **a.**
| | | × | | × | | / | | = | |

b.
(		×		×		/		)	−
(		×		×		/		)	=
	−			=	

c.
| | − | | | = | |

3. | **a.**
| | | × | | × | | / | | = | |

b.
(		×		×		/		)	−
[(| | − | | |)	×		×		/		] =
	−			=	

c.
| | − | | | = | |

E9A. Effective Interest Method

		(		×		×		/		) −	
		(		×		×		/		) =	
			−			=					
		[(		+		) ×		×			
		/	]	−	(		×		×		
		/	)	=		−					
		=									

E10A. Bond Retirement

1.

	×		=		

2.

(		/		) ×		=		
	−	(		−		)	=	

E11A. Bond Conversion

1.

2.

(　　　／　　　) × 　　　shares = 　　　shares

3.

(　　　shares × 　　　)

E12A. Effective Interest Method and Interest Accrual

			(	×	×	/	)	−		
			(	×	×	/	)	=		
			−		=					

$$[(\quad + \quad) \times \quad \times \quad / \quad] - (\quad \times \quad \times \quad / \quad) = \quad - \quad = \quad$$

E13A. Time Value of Money and Early Extinguishment of Debt

1.				
		×		
		×		

2.		

E14A. Bond Issue on and Between Interest Dates

a.									
				×	×	/		
			=					
b.									

E15A. Bond Issue Between Interest Dates

1.

				×		×		/			
		=									

				×		×		/			
		=									

2.

		×		=	

(_____ − _____) + _____ (_____)

+ _____ (_____) = _____

E16A. Year-End Accrual of Bond Interest

				×		×		/		=			
				×		×		/		=			
			−		=								

				×		×		/		=			

E17A. Recording Lease Obligations

1.

			×		=	

2.

3.

			/	years	=	

4.

			×		=	

		(		−		) ×	
		=					

E18A. Interest Coverage Ratio

Interest Coverage Ratio	=	Income Before Income Taxes + Interest Expense		
		Interest Expense		
2013	=	+		
	=	=	times*	
2014	=	+		
	=	=	times*	

*Rounded

Problems

P1. Bond Terminology

1.					
	1.		10.		
	2.		11.		
	3.		12.		
	4.		13.		
	5.		14.		
	6.		15.		
	7.		16.		
	8.		17.		
	9.				

2.	

P2. Bond Basics—Straight-Line Method, Retirement, and Conversion

1.	a.					
			$\times$		$=$	
	b.					
	c.					

d. Interest components

(1)

	$\times$		$\times$		$/$		$=$	

(2)

	$/$	$($		years	$\times$		$)$	$=$	

(3)

	$=$			$-$		$=$	

2.	a.					
			$\times$		$=$	
	b.					
	c.					

d. Interest components

(1)

	$\times$		$\times$		$/$		$=$	

(2)

	$/$	$($		years	$\times$		$)$	$=$	

(3)

	$=$			$+$		$=$	

P2. Bond Basics—Straight-Line Method, Retirement and Conversion (Concluded)

3.

a.

         =   ×   =

b.

         + (−   ) =

4.

a.

b.

         /   ×   =

c.

5.

14-21

P3. Bond Transactions—Effective Interest Method

1.

		(		×		×	/		)	−		
		(		×		×	/		)	=		
			−		=							
		(		×		×	/		)	−		
		(		×		×	/		)	=		
			−		=							

P3. Bond Transactions—Effective Interest Method

P3. Bond Transactions—Effective Interest Method (Concluded)

2.

			(		×		×	/		)	−		
			(		×		×	/		)	=		
				−		=							
			(		×		×	/		)	−		
			(		×		×	/		)	=		
				−		=							

3.

P4. Bonds Issued at a Discount and a Premium—Effective Interest Method

1.

		(		×		×	/	) −	
		(		×		×	/	)	
		=		−		=			
		(		×		×	/	) −	
		(		×		×	/	)	
		=		−		=			

14-24

P4. Bonds Issued at a Discount and a Premium—Effective Interest Method (Continued)

						×		×		/		) −			
			(			×		×		/		)			
			=		−			=							

			(			×		×		/		) −			
			(			×		×		/		)			
			=		−			=							

P4. Bonds Issued at a Discount and a Premium—Effective Interest Method (Concluded)

2.

a.

b.

c.

P5. Lease Versus Purchase

1.	a.	Present value calculated.			
			×	=	

	b.			

	c.			
		/	years	=		

	d.	Year 1			
			×	=	
	Year 2				
		(	−	) ×	
		=			

2.	a.	Month	Monthly Payment	Interest for 1 Month at 0.75% on Unpaid Balance	Reduction in Debt	Unpaid Balance at End of Period

14-27

P5. Lease Versus Purchase (Concluded)

b.

Month 1					
Month 2					

3.

Alternate Problems

P6. Bond Basics—Straight-Line Method, Retirement, and Conversion

1.

a. _____ × _____ = _____

b.

c.

d. Interest components

(1) _____ × _____ × _____ / _____ = _____

(2) _____ / (_____ years × _____) = _____

(3) _____ = _____ − _____ = _____

2.

a. _____ × _____ = _____

b.

c.

d. Interest components

(1) _____ × _____ × _____ / _____ = _____

(2) _____ / (_____ years × _____) = _____

(3) _____ = _____ + _____ = _____

3.

a. _____ × _____ = _____

b. _____ + (_____ − _____) = _____

4.

a.

b.

bonds	×	shares	=	shares

c.

| | (| | × | |) | |

| | (| shares | × | |) | |

5.

P7. Bond Transactions—Effective Interest Method

1.

			(		×		×	/	)	
			– (		×		×	/	)	
			=		–		=			
			(		×		×	/	)	
			– (		×		×	/	)	
			=		–		=			

2.

			(		×		×	/	)	
			– (		×		×	/	)	
			=		–		=			

			(		×		×	/	)	
			– (		×		×	/	)	
			=		–		=			

3.

P8. Bonds Issued at a Discount and a Premium—Effective Interest Method

1.

		(		×		×	/	) −		
		(		×		×	/	)		
		=		−		=				
		(		×		×	/	) −		
		(		×		×	/	)		
		=		−		=				
		(		×		×	/	) −		
		(		×		×	/	)		
		=		−		=				

P8. Bonds Issued at a Discount and a Premium—Effective Interest Method (Concluded)

			(		×		×		/		) −
			(		×		×		/		)
			=		−		=				
			(		×		×		/		) −
			(		×		×		/		)
			=		−		=				

2.

a.

b.

c.

P9. Lease Versus Purchase

1.

a.

	×		=	

b.

c.

	/	years	=

d.

	×	=

(−) ×

=

2.

a.

Month	Monthly Payment	Interest for 1 Month at 0.75% on Unpaid Balance	Reduction in Debt	Unpaid Balance at End of Period

P9. Lease Versus Purchase (Concluded)

b.

3.

THE STATEMENT OF CASH FLOWS

Short Exercises

SE1. Classification of Cash Flow Transactions

1.		4.	
2.		5.	
3.		6.	

SE2. Computing Cash Flows from Operating Activities: Indirect Method

SE3. Computing Cash Flows from Operating Activities: Indirect Method

SE4. Cash Flows from Investing Activities and Noncash Transactions

Note: Under the indirect method, the gain of $75,000 would appear as a deduction in the cash flows from operating activities section.

SE5. Cash Flows from Financing Activities

Note: Interest paid appears in the cash flows from operating activities section.

SE6. Identifying Components of the Statement of Cash Flows

1.		5.	
2.		6.	
3.		7.	
4.		8.	

SE7. Cash-Generating Efficiency Ratios and Free Cash Flow

Cash Flow Yield	=	Net Cash Flows from Operating Activities	
		Net Income	

	=		=	times

Cash Flows to Sales	=	Net Cash Flows from Operating Activities	
		Sales	

	=		=	

Cash Flows to Assets	=	Net Cash Flows from Operating Activities	
		Average Total Assets	

	=				=	
		(	+	) /		

Free Cash Flow	=	Net Cash Flows from Operating Activities – Dividends –
		Purchases of Plant Assets + Sales of Plant Assets

	=		–		–		+	
	=							

SE8. Cash-Generating Efficiency Ratios and Free Cash Flow

Exercises: Set A

E1A. Classification of Cash Flow Transactions

1.		6.		11.	
2.		7.		12.	
3.		8.		13.	
4.		9.			
5.		10.			

E2A. Cash Flows from Operating Activities: Indirect Method

E3A. Computing Cash Flows from Operating Activities: Indirect Method

E4A. Preparing a Schedule of Cash Flows from Operating Activities: Indirect Method

E5A. Computing Cash Flows from Investing Activities: Investments

a.		
b.		

E6A. Computing Cash Flows from Investing Activities: Plant Assets

a.			
b.			

E7A. Determining Cash Flows from Financing Activities: Notes Payable

Note: Interest Expense of $1,000 would be included in the operating activities section and would not have to be adjusted further.

E8A. Preparing the Statement of Cash Flows: Indirect Method

E9A. Cash-Generating Efficiency Ratios and Free Cash Flow

Cash Flow Yield	=	$\dfrac{\text{Net Cash Flows from Operating Activities}}{\text{Net Income}}$		
	=	_____ =		times*

Cash Flows to Sales	=	$\dfrac{\text{Net Cash Flows from Operating Activities}}{\text{Sales}}$		
	=	_____ =		*

Cash Flows to Assets	=	$\dfrac{\text{Net Cash Flows from Operating Activities}}{\text{Average Total Assets}}$		
	=	_____ (_____ + _____) / _____ =		*

Free Cash Flow	=	Net Cash Flows from Operating Activities – Dividends – Purchases of Plant Assets + Sales of Plant Assets
	=	_____ – _____ – _____ + _____
	=	_____

*Rounded

Problems

P1. Classification of Cash Flow Transactions

Transaction	Cash Flow Classification				Effect on Cash Flows		
	Operating Activity	Investing Activity	Financing Activity	Noncash Transaction	Increase	Decrease	No Effect
1. Paid a cash dividend.							
2. Decreased accounts receivable.							
3. Increased inventory.							
4. Incurred a net loss.							
5. Declared and issued a stock dividend.							
6. Retired long-term debt with cash.							
7. Sold available-for-sale securities at a loss.							
8. Issued stock for equipment.							
9. Decreased prepaid insurance.							
10. Purchased treasury stock with cash.							
11. Retired a fully depreciated truck (no gain or loss).							
12. Increased interest payable.							
13. Decreased dividends receivable on investment.							
14. Sold treasury stock.							
15. Increased income taxes payable.							
16. Transferred cash to money market account.				*			
17. Purchased land and building with a mortgage.							

*Cash equivalent

15-10

P2. Interpreting and Analyzing the Statement of Cash Flows

1.

2. Free Cash Flow

2013:		−		−		=	
2014:		−		−		=	

3.

4.

P3. Statement of Cash Flows: Indirect Method

1.

P3. Statement of Cash Flows: Indirect Method (Concluded)

2.

3.

Cash Flow Yield	=	Net Cash Flows from Operating Activities	
		Net Income	

	=		=		times*

Free Cash Flow	=	Net Cash Flows from Operating Activities – Dividends –
		Purchases of Plant Assets + Sales of Plant Assets

	=		–		–		+		

	=	

*Rounded

P4. Statement of Cash Flows: Indirect Method

1.

P4. Statement of Cash Flows: Indirect Method (Concluded)

2.

3.

Cash Flow Yield	=	Net Cash Flows from Operating Activities
		Net Income

	=		=	not meaningful

Free Cash Flow	=	Net Cash Flows from Operating Activities – Dividends –
		Net Capital Expenditures

	=		–		–	

	=		

P5. Statement of Cash Flows: Indirect Method

1.

P5. Statement of Cash Flows: Indirect Method (Concluded)

2.

3.

Cash Flow Yield	=	Net Cash Flows from Operating Activities		
		Net Income		

2014	=		=		times*

Free Cash Flow	=	Net Cash Flows from Operating Activities – Dividends –		
		Purchases of Plant Assets + Sales of Plant Assets		

2014	=		–		–		+	
	=							

*Rounded

Alternate Problems

P6. Classification of Cash Flow Transactions

Transaction	Cash Flow Classification				Effect on Cash Flows		
	Operating Activity	Investing Activity	Financing Activity	Noncash Transaction	Increase	Decrease	No Effect
1. Increased accounts payable.							
2. Decreased inventory.							
3. Increased prepaid insurance.							
4. Earned a net income.							
5. Declared and paid a cash dividend.							
6. Issued stock for cash.							
7. Retired long-term debt by issuing stock.							
8. Purchased a long-term investment with cash.							
9. Sold trading securities at a gain.							
10. Sold a machine at a loss.							
11. Retired fully depreciated equipment.							
12. Decreased interest payable.							
13. Purchased available-for-sale securities (long-term).							
14. Decreased dividends receivable.							
15. Decreased accounts receivable.							
16. Converted bonds to common stock.							
17. Purchased 90-day Treasury bill.				*			

*Cash equivalent

15-18

P7. Statement of Cash Flows: Indirect Method

1.

2.

a.

b.

c.

d.

e.

P7. Statement of Cash Flows: Indirect Method (Concluded)

3.

	Cash Flow Yield	=	Net Cash Flows from Operating Activities	
			Net Income	
		=		=	times*

	Free Cash Flow	=	Net Cash Flows from Operating Activities – Dividends –
			Purchases of Plant Assets + Sales of Plant Assets
		=	−	−	+
		=	

*Rounded

P8. Statement of Cash Flows: Indirect Method

1.

P8. Statement of Cash Flows: Indirect Method (Concluded)

2.

3.

Cash Flow Yield	=	Net Cash Flows from Operating Activities	
		Net Income	
	=		=	times*

Free Cash Flow	=	Net Cash Flows from Operating Activities – Dividends –
		Purchases of Plant Assets + Sales of Plant Assets
	=	– – +
	=	

*Rounded

P9. Statement of Cash Flows: Indirect Method

1.

2.

3.

Cash Flow Yield	=	Net Cash Flows from Operating Activities
		Net Income

	=		=	not meaningful

Free Cash Flow	=	Net Cash Flows from Operating Activities – Dividends –
		Net Capital Expenditures

	=		–		–	
	=					

P10. Statement of Cash Flows: Indirect Method

1.

P10. Statement of Cash Flows: Indirect Method (Concluded)

2.

3.

Cash Flow Yield	=	Net Cash Flows from Operating Activities
		Net Income

2014	=		=		times*

Free Cash Flow	=	Net Cash Flows from Operating Activities – Dividends –
		Purchases of Plant Assets + Sales of Plant Assets

2014	=		–		–		+		
	=								

*Rounded

CHAPTER 15 SUPPLEMENT—Working Papers
THE DIRECT METHOD OF PREPARING THE STATEMENT OF CASH FLOWS

Short Exercises

SE1. Cash Receipts from Sales and Cash Payments for Purchases: Direct Method

Cash Receipts from Sales	=	Sales	+	Decrease in Accounts Receivable –
	=		+	( )
	=		+	

Cash Payments for Purchases	=	Cost of Goods Sold	+	Increase in Inventory –	+	Decrease in Accounts Payable –
	=		+	( )	+	( )
	=		+		+	

SE2. Cash Payments for Operating Expenses and Income Taxes: Direct Method

Cash Payments for Operating Expenses	=	Operating Expenses	–	Decrease in Prepaid Expenses –	+	Decrease in Accrued Liabilities –	–	Depreciation Expense
	=		–	( )	+	( )	–	
	=		–		+		–	

Cash Payments for Income Taxes	=	Income Taxes Expense	+	Decrease in Income Taxes Payable –
	=		+	( )
	=		+	

15S-1

Exercises

E1. Computing Cash flows from Operating Activities: Direct Method

a.

Cash Receipts from Sales	=	Cash Sales	+	Credit Sales	+	Decrease in Accounts Receivable
	=		+		+	
	=					

b.

Cash Payments for Purchases	=	Cost of Goods Sold	+	Increase in Inventory	+	Decrease in Accounts Payable
	=		+		+	
	=					

c.

Cash Payments for Operating Expenses	=	Operating Expenses	–	Decrease in Prepaid Expenses	–	Increase in Accrued Liabilities	–	Depreciation Expense
	=		–		–		–	
	=							

d.

Cash Payments for Income Taxes	=	Income Taxes Expense	+	Decrease in Income Taxes Payable
	=		+	
	=			

E2. **Preparing a Schedule of Cash Flows from Operating Activities: Direct Method**

(a)	**Cash Receipts from Sales**	**=**	**Sales**	**−**	**Increase in Accounts Receivable**	
		=		−		
		=				

(b)	**Cash Payments for Purchases**	**=**	**Cost of Goods Sold**	**+**	**Increase in Inventories**	**−**	**Increase in Accounts Payable**	
		=		+		−		
		=						

(c)	**Cash Payments for Operating Expenses**	**=**	**Operating Expenses**	**−**	**Decrease in Prepaid Rent**	**−**	**Increase in Salaries Payable**	**−**	**Depreciation Expense**
		=		−		−		−	
		=							

(d)	**Cash Payments for Income Taxes**	**=**	**Income Taxes Expense**	**+**	**Decrease in Income Taxes Payable**	
		=		+		
		=				

Problems

P1. Cash Flows from Operating Activities: Direct Method

(a)	Cash Receipts from Sales	=	Sales	−	Increase in Accounts Receivable				
		=		−					
		=							

(b)	Cash Payments for Purchases	=	Cost of Goods Sold	+	Increase in Inventories	−	Increase in Accounts Payable		
		=		+		−			
		=							

(c)	Cash Payments for Operating Expenses	=	Operating Expenses	+	Increase in Prepaid Expenses	+	Decrease in Accrued Liabilities		
		=		+		+			
			−	Depreciation and Amortization					
			−		+				
		=							

(d)	Cash Payments for Income Taxes	=	Income Taxes Expense	+	Decrease in Income Taxes Payable				
				+					
		=							

P2. Statement of Cash Flows: Direct Method

1.

(a)	Cash Receipts from Sales	=	Sales	+	Decrease in Accounts Receivable	
		=		+		
		=				

(b)	Cash Payments for Purchases	=	Cost of Goods Sold	−	Decrease in Inventory	−	Increase in Accounts Payable
		=		−		−	
		=					

(c)	Cash Payments for Operating Expenses	=	Operating Expenses	−	Decrease in Prepaid Expenses	−	Depreciation
		=		−		−	
		=					

(d)	Cash Payments for Income Taxes	=	Income Tax Expense	−	Increase in Income Taxes Payable	
		=		−		
		=				

15S-5

P2. Statement of Cash Flows: Direct Method (Continued)

(e)

(f)

(g)

(h)

(i)

(j)

2.

P2. Statement of Cash Flows: Direct Method (Concluded)

3.

Cash Flow Yield	=	Net Cash Flows from Operating Activities
		Net Income

	=		=		times*

Free Cash Flow	=	Net Cash Flows from Operating Activities	–	Dividends	–	Net Capital Expenditures
	=		–		–	+
	=					

*Rounded

P3. Statement of Cash Flows: Direct Method

1.

(a)	Cash Receipts from Sales	=	Sales	+	Decrease in Accounts Receivable			
		=		+				
		=						
(b)	Cash Payments for Purchases	=	Cost of Goods Sold	−	Decrease in Inventory	−	Increase in Accounts Payable	
		=		−		−		
		=						
(c)	Cash Payments for Operating Expenses	=	Operating Expenses	−	Decrease in Prepaid Expenses	−	Depreciation	
		=		−		−		
		=						
(d)	Cash Payments for Income Taxes	=	Income Tax Expense	−	Increase in Income Taxes Payable			
		=		−				
		=						

15S-8

P3. Statement of Cash Flows: Direct Method (Continued)

(e)

(f)

(g)

(h)

(i)

(j)

2.

P3. Statement of Cash Flows: Direct Method (Concluded)

3.	Cash Flow Yield	=	Net Cash Flows from Operating Activities		
			Net Income		
		=		=	times*

	Free Cash Flow	=	Net Cash Flows from Operating Activities	–	Dividends	–	Net Capital Expenditures
		=		–		–	+
		=					

*Rounded

FINANCIAL STATEMENT ANALYSIS

SE1. Objectives and Standards of Financial Performance Evaluation

1.			4.	
2.			5.	
3.			6.	

SE2. Sources of Information

1.			4.	
2.			5.	
3.				

SE3. Trend Analysis

	2014	2013	2012

SE4. Horizontal Analysis

	2014	2013	Increase or Decrease	
			Amount	Percentage

SE5. Vertical Analysis

Assets	2014	2013
Liabilities and Stockholders' Equity		

SE6. Operating Asset Management Analysis

	2014	2013

Current ratio:

$$\frac{\text{Current Assets}}{\text{Current Liabilities}} = \underline{\quad} = \underline{\quad}\text{ times*} \qquad = \underline{\quad} = \underline{\quad}\text{ time*}$$

Quick ratio:

$$\frac{\text{Cash} + \text{Marketable Securities} + \text{Receivables}}{\text{Current Liabilities}} = \frac{\underline{\quad} + \underline{\quad} + \underline{\quad}}{\underline{\quad}} = \underline{\quad}\text{ time*} \qquad = \frac{\underline{\quad} + \underline{\quad} + \underline{\quad}}{\underline{\quad}} = \underline{\quad}\text{ time*}$$

Receivables turnover:

$$\frac{\text{Net Sales}}{\text{Average Accounts Receivable}} = \frac{\underline{\quad}}{(\underline{\quad} + \underline{\quad})/\underline{\quad}} = \underline{\quad}\text{ times} \qquad = \frac{\underline{\quad}}{(\underline{\quad} + \underline{\quad})/\underline{\quad}} = \underline{\quad}\text{ times*}$$

Days' sales uncollected:

$$\frac{\text{Days in Year}}{\text{Receivable Turnover}} = \frac{\underline{\quad}\text{ days}}{\underline{\quad}\text{ times}} = \underline{\quad}\text{ days*} \qquad = \frac{\underline{\quad}\text{ days}}{\underline{\quad}\text{ times}} = \underline{\quad}\text{ days*}$$

*Rounded

16-4

SE6. Operating Asset Management Analysis (Concluded)

	2014				2013			
Inventory turnover:								
Cost of Goods Sold								
Average Inventory	= (	+	) /	times*	= (	+	) /	times*
Days' inventory on hand:								
Days in Year								
Inventory Turnover	=			days*	=			days*
Payables turnover:								
Cost of Goods Sold +/–								
Change in Inventories		+				+		
Average								
Accounts Payable	= (	+	) /	times*	= (	+	) /	times*
Days' payable:								
Days in Year	days	=		days*	days	=		days*
Payables Turnover	times				times			
Financing period:								
Days' inventory on hand	days	=		days	days	=		days
Days' sales uncollected	+ days				+ days			
Days' payable	– days				– days			

*Rounded

SE7. Profitability and Total Asset Management Analysis

Profit margin:

	2014			2013	
Net Income					
————	=			=	
Net Sales					

Asset turnover:

	2014			2013	
Net Sales					
————————	=	(	+	) /	(	+	) /
Average Total Assets					
	=			=	
	=	times*		=	times*

Return on assets:

	2014			2013	
Net Income					
————————	=			=	
Average Total Assets					

*Rounded

16-6

SE8. Financial Risk Analysis

Debt to equity ratio:

	2014				2013			
Total Liabilities	=	___ + ___	=	times*	=	___ + ___	=	times*
Stockholders' Equity								

Return on equity:

	2014				2013			
Net Income	=	(___ + ___) / ___			=	(___ + ___) / ___		
Average Stockholders' Equity	=				=			

Interest coverage ratio:

	2014				2013			
Income Before Income								
Taxes + Interest Expense	=	___ + ___	=	times	=	___ + ___	=	times
Interest Expense								

*Rounded

16-7

SE9. Liquidity Analysis

	2014	2013
Cash flow yield:		
Net Cash Flows from Operating Activities		
Net Income	= _____ times*	= _____ times
Cash flows to sales:		
Net Cash Flows from Operating Activities		
Net Sales	= _____	= _____
Cash flows to assets:		
Net Cash Flows from Operating Activities		
Average Total Assets	= _____ / (_____ + _____) /	= _____ / (_____ + _____) /
	= _____	= _____
Free cash flow:		
Net Cash Flows from Operating Activities – Dividends – Net Capital Expenditures	= _____ – _____ – _____	= _____ – _____ – _____
	= _____	= _____

*Rounded

16-8

SE10. Market Strength Analysis

Price/earnings (P/E) ratio:

	2014		2013	
Market Price per Share				
───────────────────	=	times*	=	times*
Earnings per Share				

Dividend yield:

	2014		2013	
Dividends per Share**				
───────────────────	=		=	
Market Price per Share				

*Rounded

SE11. Quality of Earnings

1.
2.
3.
4.
5.
6.
7.

SE12. Corporate Income Statement

Exercises: Set A

E1A. Issues in Financial Performance Evaluation: Objectives, Standards, Sources of Information, and Executive Compensation

1.		6.	
2.		7.	
3.		8.	
4.		9.	
5.		10.	

E2A. Trend Analysis

	2014	2013	2012	2011	2010

E3A. Horizontal Analysis

	2014	2013	Increase or Decrease	
			Amount	Percentage*
Assets				
Liabilities and Stockholders' Equity				

*Rounded

E4A. Vertical Analysis

	2014	2013

E5A. Operating Asset Management Analysis

	2014				2013			
Current ratio	———	=		times		———	=		times
Quick ratio		+		+			+		+	
	———					———				
	=		times*			=		times*		
Receivables turnover	———					———				
	(	+		) /		(	+		) /	
	=	———	=		times*	=	———	=		times*
Days' sales uncollected	days / times	=		days*		days / times	=		days*	
Inventory turnover	———					———				
	(	+		) /		(	+		) /	
	=	———	=		times*	=	———	=		times*
Days' inventory on hand	days / times	=		days*		days / times	=		days*	
Payables turnover		+					−			
	———					———				
	(	+		) /		(	+		) /	
	=	———	=		times*	=	———	=		times*
Days' payable	days / times	=		days*		days / times	=		days*	
Financing period	days	+		−		days	+	days	−	
	days	=				days	=	days		

*Rounded

E6A. Turnover Analysis

(amounts in thousands)

	Receivables Turnover*	Inventory Turnover*	Payables Turnover*
	Net Sales	Cost of Goods Sold	Cost of Goods Sold +/– Change in Inventory
	Average Accounts Receivable	Average Inventory	Average Accounts Payable
Year			
2011	(___) / [(___ + ___)] = ___ times	(___) / [(___ + ___)] = ___ times	___ – [(___ + ___)] / (___) = ___ times
2012	(___) / [(___ + ___)] = ___ times	(___) / [(___ + ___)] = ___ times	___ + [(___ + ___)] / (___) = ___ times
2013	(___) / [(___ + ___)] = ___ times	(___) / [(___ + ___)] = ___ times	___ + [(___ + ___)] / (___) = ___ times
2014	(___) / [(___ + ___)] = ___ times	(___) / [(___ + ___)] = ___ times	___ + [(___ + ___)] / (___) = ___ times

*Rounded

E7A. Profitability and Total Asset Management Analysis

	2014			2013		
Profit margin*	_____ =		_____	_____ =		_____
Asset turnover*	(_____ + _____) /			(_____ + _____) /		
	= _____ =		times	= _____ =		times
Return on assets*	(_____ + _____) /			(_____ + _____) /		
	= _____ =			= _____ =		

*Rounded

E8A. Financial Risk and Market Strength Ratios

	Company A			Company B		
Debt to equity ratio*	_____	=	time	_____	=	times
	_____	−		_____	−	
Return on equity*	(_____	+	) /	(_____	+	) /
	= _____	=		= _____	=	
Interest coverage ratio*	_____ + _____			_____ + _____		
	=	times		=	times	
Price/earnings (P/E) ratio	= _____	=	times	= _____	=	times
Dividend yield	_____	=		_____	=	

*Rounded

E9A. Liquidity Analysis

Cash flow yield		=		times*

Cash flows to sales	=	=	

Cash flows to assets	(	+	) /
	=	=	

Free cash flow	=	−	−	=

*Rounded

E10A. Effect of Alternative Accounting Methods

1.

(−)

2.

(−)

3.

4.

5.

E11A. Corporate Income Statement

E12A. Corporate Income Statement

Problems

P1. Horizontal and Vertical Analysis

1.

			Increase or Decrease	
	2014	**2013**	**Amount**	**Percentage***

*Rounded

P1. Horizontal and Vertical Analysis (Continued)

	2014	2013	Increase or Decrease	
			Amount	Percentage*
Assets				
Liabilities and Stockholders' Equity				

*Rounded

2.

	2014*	2013*

	2014*	2013*
Assets		
Liabilities and Stockholders' Equity		

* Rounded. In common-size statements, the addition and subtraction of percentages are sometimes inexact due to rounding.

P1. Horizontal and Vertical Analysis (Concluded)

3.

P2. Effects of Transactions on Ratios

Transaction		Ratio	Effect		
			Increase	Decrease	None
a.	Issued common stock for cash.	Asset turnover			
b.	Declared cash dividend.	Current ratio			
c.	Sold treasury stock.	Return on equity			
d.	Borrowed cash by issuing note payable.	Debt to equity ratio			
e.	Paid salaries expense.	Inventory turnover			
f.	Purchased merchandise for cash.	Current ratio			
g.	Sold equipment for cash.	Receivables turnover			
h.	Sold merchandise on account.	Quick ratio			
i.	Paid current portion of long-term debt.	Return on assets			
j.	Gave sales discount.	Profit margin			
k.	Purchased marketable securities for cash.	Quick ratio			
l.	Declared 5% stock dividend.	Current ratio			
m.	Purchased a building.	Free cash flow			

P3. Comprehensive Ratio Analysis

	Ratio	2014	2013	6. Favorable (F) or Unfavorable (U) Change
1.	Operating asset management analysis			
a.	Current ratio*	___ + ___ ____ = ____ + ____ ___ + ___ = ____ times	___ + ___ ____ = ____ + ____ ___ + ___ = ____ times	Neutral
b.	Quick ratio*	___ + ___ ___ + ___ ____ = _____ = ____ time	___ + ___ ___ + ___ ____ = _____ = ____ time	Neutral
c.	Receivables turnover*	(___ + ___) / _____ = ____ times	(___ + ___) / _____ = ____ times	U
d.	Days' sales uncollected*	____ days _____ = ____ days ____ times	____ days _____ = ____ days ____ times	U

*Rounded

Note: These analyses indicate the apparently favorable or unfavorable change in each ratio. Class discussion may focus on conditions that might lead to different conclusions.

Note: All amounts used in calculating the ratios and percentages are in thousands of dollars, except the amounts used to calculate the P/E ratio and the dividend yield.

16-25

P3. Comprehensive Ratio Analysis (Continued)

Ratio	2014	2013	6. Favorable (F) or Unfavorable (U) Change
e. Inventory turnover*	(＿ + ＿) / ＿ = ＿ times	(＿ + ＿) / ＿ = ＿ times	Neutral
f. Days' inventory on hand*	＿ days / ＿ times = ＿ days	＿ days / ＿ times = ＿ days	F
g. Payables turnover*	(＿ + ＿) / ＿ = ＿ times	(＿ + ＿) / ＿ = ＿ times	U
h. Days' payable*	＿ days / ＿ times = ＿ days	＿ days / ＿ times = ＿ days	U
i. Financing period	＿ days − ＿ days = ＿ days	＿ days − ＿ days = ＿ days	F

*Rounded

P3. Comprehensive Ratio Analysis (Continued)

	Ratio	2014	2013	6. Favorable (F) or Unfavorable (U) Change
2.	**Profitability and total asset management analysis**			
a.	Profit margin*	——— =	——— =	U
b.	Asset turnover*	(————) = ————— + ————— / ————— times =	(————) = ————— + ————— / ————— times =	Neutral
c.	Return on assets*	(————) = ————— + ————— / ————— =	(————) = ————— + ————— / ————— =	U

*Rounded

16-27

P3. Comprehensive Ratio Analysis (Continued)

Ratio	2014	2013	6. Favorable (F) or Unfavorable (U) Change
3. Financial risk analysis			
a. Debt to equity ratio*	___ = ___ + ___ + ___ time	___ = ___ + ___ + ___ time	U
b. Return on equity*	(___) / ___ = ___ + ___	(___) / ___ = ___ + ___	U
c. Interest coverage ratio*	___ = ___ + ___ times	___ = ___ + ___ times	U

*Rounded

P3. Comprehensive Ratio Analysis (Continued)

Ratio	2014	2013	6. Favorable (F) or Unfavorable (U) Change
4. Liquidity analysis			
a. Cash flow yield*	___ = ___ times	___ = ___ times	F
b. Cash flows to sales*	___ = ___	___ = ___	U
c. Cash flows to assets*	(___ + ___) / ___ = ___	(___ + ___) / ___ = ___	U
d. Free cash flow	___ - ___ - ___ = ___	___ - ___ - ___ = ___	U

*Rounded

P3. Comprehensive Ratio Analysis (Concluded)

	Ratio	2014			2013			6. Favorable (F) or Unfavorable (U) Change
5.	Market strength analysis							
a.	Price/earnings (P/E) ratio*	___ / ___ = ___ times			___ / ___ = ___ times			F
b.	Dividend yield*	___ / ___ = ___ = ___ shares			___ / ___ = ___ = ___ shares			F

*Rounded

P4. Comprehensive Ratio Analysis of Two Companies

	Ratio Name	Single	Design	6. Company with More Favorable Ratio
1.	Operating asset management analysis			
a.	Current ratio*	__ = __ + __ + __ = __ + __ times	__ = __ + __ + __ = __ + __ times	Single
b.	Quick ratio*	__ = __ + __ + __ = __ times	__ = __ + __ + __ = __ times	Single
c.	Receivables turnover*	__ = __ times	__ = __ times	Design
d.	Days' sales uncollected*	__ days = __ = __ times days	__ days = __ = __ times days	Design

*Rounded

16-31

P4. Comprehensive Ratio Analysis of Two Companies (Continued)

Ratio Name	Single	Design	6. Company with More Favorable Ratio
e. Inventory turnover*	――― = ――― times	――― = ――― times	Design
f. Days' inventory on hand*	――― days = ――― days ――― times	――― days = ――― days ――― times	Design
g. Payables turnover*	――― + ――― = ――― times	――― + ――― = ――― times	Design
h. Days' payable*	――― days = ――― days ――― times	――― days = ――― days ――― times	Design
i. Financing period	――― days + ――― days – ――― days = ――― days	――― days + ――― days – ――― days = ――― days	Design

*Rounded

P4. Comprehensive Ratio Analysis of Two Companies (Continued)

Ratio Name	Single	Design	6. Company with More Favorable Ratio
2. Profitability and total asset management analysis			
a. Profit margin*	___ =	___ =	Single
b. Asset turnover*	___ = ___ times	___ = ___ times	Design
c. Return on assets*	___ =	___ =	Single

*Rounded

16-33

P4. Comprehensive Ratio Analysis of Two Companies (Continued)

	Ratio Name	Single	Design	6. Company with More Favorable Ratio
3.	Financial risk analysis			
a.	Debt to equity ratio*	+ + + = + + = time	+ + + = + + = time	Design
b.	Return on equity*	+ = + =	+ = + =	Single
c.	Interest coverage ratio*	+ = times =	+ = times =	Design

*Rounded

16-34

P4. Comprehensive Ratio Analysis of Two Companies (Continued)

	Ratio Name	Single	Design	6. Company with More Favorable Ratio
4.	Liquidity analysis			
a.	Cash flow yield*	= ___ times	= ___ times	Design
b.	Cash flows to sales*	= ___	= ___	Single
c.	Cash flows to assets*	= ___	= ___	Neutral
d.	Free cash flow	= ___ - ___ - ___	= ___ - ___ - ___	Single

*Rounded

Ratio Name	Single	Design	6. Company with More Favorable Ratio
5. Market strength analysis			
a. Price/earnings (P/E) ratio*	_____ = _____ times	_____ = _____ times	Single
b. Dividend yield*	_____ / _____ shares = _____	_____ / _____ shares = _____	Design
*Rounded			
7.			

P5. Effect of Alternative Accounting Methods

1.

		/	years			
		×				

P5. Effect of Alternative Accounting Methods (Continued)

2.

3.

Inventory Turnover	FIFO Method		LIFO Method	
Cost of Goods Sold ─────────── Ending Inventory	────── =	times*	────── =	times*

*Rounded

P5. Effect of Alternative Accounting Methods (Concluded)

4. Return on Assets

		FIFO/Straight-Line Methods					
Net Income	=						
Total Assets			+		+		−
	=		=				

		LIFO/Double-Declining-Balance Methods					
	=						
			+		+		−
	=		=				

P6. Corporate Income Statement

1.

2.

Alternate Problems

P7. Horizontal and Vertical Analysis

1.

	2014	2013	Increase or Decrease	
			Amount	Percentage*

*Rounded

P7. Horizontal and Vertical Analysis (Continued)

	2014	2013	Increase or Decrease	
			Amount	Percentage*
Assets				
Liabilities and Stockholders' Equity				

*Rounded

P7. Horizontal and Vertical Analysis (Continued)

2.

				2014*	2013*

			2014*	2013*
Assets				
Liabilities and Stockholders' Equity				

* Rounded. In common-size statements, the addition and subtraction of percentages are sometimes inexact due to rounding.

3.

	P8. Effects of Transactions on Ratios				
				Effect	
	Transaction	Ratio	Increase	Decrease	None
a.	Sold merchandise on account.	Current ratio			
b.	Sold merchandise on account.	Inventory turnover			
c.	Collected on accounts receivable.	Quick ratio			
d.	Wrote off an uncollectible account.	Receivables turnover			
e.	Paid on accounts payable.	Current ratio			
f.	Declared cash dividend.	Return on equity			
g.	Incurred advertising expense.	Profit margin			
h.	Issued stock dividend.	Debt to equity ratio			
i.	Issued bonds payable.	Asset turnover			
j.	Accrued interest expense.	Current ratio			
k.	Paid previously declared cash dividend.	Dividend yield			
l.	Purchased treasury stock.	Return on assets			
m.	Recorded depreciation expense.	Cash flow yield			

P9. Comprehensive Ratio Analysis

	Ratio Name	2014	2013	6. Favorable (F) or Unfavorable (U) Change
1.	Operating asset management analysis			
a.	Current ratio*	$\dfrac{\quad + \quad + \quad}{\quad + \quad} = \quad$ times	$\dfrac{\quad + \quad + \quad}{\quad + \quad} = \quad$ time	F
b.	Quick ratio*	$\dfrac{\quad + \quad + \quad}{\quad} = \quad$ time	$\dfrac{\quad + \quad + \quad}{\quad} = \quad$ time	F
c.	Receivables turnover*	$\dfrac{\quad}{(\quad + \quad) / \quad} = \quad$ times	$\dfrac{\quad}{(\quad + \quad) / \quad} = \quad$ times	U
d.	Days' sales uncollected*	$\dfrac{\quad \text{days}}{\quad \text{times}} = \quad$ days	$\dfrac{\quad \text{days}}{\quad \text{times}} = \quad$ days	U

*Rounded

Note: These analyses indicate the apparently favorable or unfavorable change in each ratio. Class discussion may focus on conditions that might lead to different conclusions.

Note: All amounts used in calculating the ratios and percentages are in thousands of dollars, except the amounts used to calculate the P/E ratio and the dividends yield.

16-46

P9. Comprehensive Ratio Analysis (Continued)

	Ratio Name	2014	2013	6. Favorable (F) or Unfavorable (U) Change
e.	Inventory turnover*	(+) / = times	(+) / = times	Neutral
f.	Days' inventory on hand*	days / times = days	= days	F
g.	Payables turnover*	(+ −) / = times	(+ +) / = times	F
h.	Days' payable*	days / times = days	days / times = days	F
i.	Financing period	days + days − days = days	days + days − days = days	U

*Rounded

P9. Comprehensive Ratio Analysis (Continued)

Ratio Name	2014	2013	6. Favorable (F) or Unfavorable (U) Change
2. Profitability and total asset management analysis			
a. Profit margin*	= ____ =	= ____ =	F
b. Asset turnover*	= (____ + ____) = ____ times	= (____ + ____) = ____ times	Neutral
c. Return on assets*	= (____ + ____) =	= (____ + ____) =	F

*Rounded

16-48

P9. Comprehensive Ratio Analysis (Continued)

	Ratio Name	2014	2013	6. Favorable (F) or Unfavorable (U) Change
3.	Financial risk analysis			
a.	Debt to equity ratio*	= ____ + ____ + ____ = ____ times	= ____ + ____ + ____ = ____ times	Neutral
b.	Return on equity*	= (____ + ____) / = ____	= (____ + ____) / = ____	F
c.	Interest coverage ratio*	= ____ + ____ = ____ times	= ____ + ____ = ____ times	U

*Rounded

	Ratio Name	2014	2013	6. Favorable (F) or Unfavorable (U) Change
4.	**Liquidity analysis**			
a.	Cash flow yield*	___ / ___ = ___	___ / ___ = ___ times	U
b.	Cash flows to sales*	___ / ___ = ___	___ / ___ = ___	U
c.	Cash flows to assets*	(___ + ___) / ___ = ___	(___ + ___) / ___ = ___	U
d.	Free cash flows	___ - ___ - ___ = ___	___ - ___ - ___ = ___	U
5.	**Market strength analysis**			
a.	Price/earnings (P/E) ratio*	___ / ___ = ___ times	___ / ___ = ___ times	U
b.	Dividend yield*	___ / ___ shares = ___	___ / ___ shares = ___	F

*Rounded

16-50

P10. Comprehensive Ratio Analysis of Two Companies

Ratio Name		Lucent	Ranbaxy	6. Company with More Favorable Ratio
1.	Operating asset management analysis			
a.	Current ratio*	$\dfrac{\_\_+\_\_+\_\_}{\_\_+\_\_} = \_\_\_\_ =$ ___ times	$\dfrac{\_\_+\_\_+\_\_}{\_\_+\_\_} = \_\_\_\_ =$ ___ times	Lucent
b.	Quick ratio*	$\dfrac{\_\_+\_\_}{\_\_+\_\_} = \_\_\_\_ =$ ___ times	$\dfrac{\_\_+\_\_}{\_\_+\_\_} = \_\_\_\_ =$ ___ times	Lucent
c.	Receivables turnover*	$\dfrac{\_\_}{\_\_} =$ ___ times	$\dfrac{\_\_}{\_\_} =$ ___ times	Ranbaxy
d.	Days' sales uncollected*	$\dfrac{\text{days}}{\text{times}} =$ ___ days	$\dfrac{\text{days}}{\text{times}} =$ ___ days	Ranbaxy

*Rounded

16-51

P10. Comprehensive Ratio Analysis of Two Companies (Continued)

	Ratio Name	Lucent	Ranbaxy	6. Company with More Favorable Ratio
e.	Inventory turnover*	___ = times	___ = times	Ranbaxy
f.	Days' inventory on hand*	days / times = days	days / times = days	Ranbaxy
g.	Payables turnover*	___ + ___ = times	___ + ___ = times	Lucent
h.	Days' payable*	days / times = days	days / times = days	Lucent
i.	Financing period	days + days − days = days	days + days − days = days	Ranbaxy

*Rounded

16-52

P10. Comprehensive Ratio Analysis of Two Companies (Continued)

	Ratio Name	Lucent		Ranbaxy		6. Company with More Favorable Ratio
2.	Profitability and total asset management analysis					
a.	Profit margin*		=		=	Lucent
b.	Asset turnover*		= times		= times	Ranbaxy
c.	Return on assets*		=		=	Lucent
	*Rounded					

Ratio Name	Lucent	Ranbaxy	6. Company with More Favorable Ratio
3. Financial risk analysis			
a. Debt to equity ratio*	+ = + + time	+ = + + time	Ranbaxy
b. Return on equity*	+ = +	+ = +	Lucent
c. Interest coverage ratio*	+ = times	+ = times	Ranbaxy

*Rounded

16-54

P10. Comprehensive Ratio Analysis of Two Companies (Continued)

Ratio Name	Lucent	Ranbaxy	6. Company with More Favorable Ratio
4. Liquidity analysis			
a. Cash flow yield*	———— = ———— times	———— = ———— times	Ranbaxy
b. Cash flows to sales*	———— = ————	———— = ————	Lucent
c. Cash flows to assets*	———— = ————	———— = ————	Neutral
d. Free cash flow	— — — = —	— — — = —	Lucent

*Rounded

16-55

P10. Comprehensive Ratio Analysis of Two Companies (Concluded)

Ratio Name	Lucent		Ranbaxy		6. Company with More Favorable Ratio
5. Market strength analysis					
a. Price/earnings (P/E) ratio*	___ = ___	times	___ = ___	times	Lucent
b. Dividend yield*	___ / ___ shares = ___ = ___		___ / ___ shares = ___ = ___		Ranbaxy
*Rounded					
7.					

P11. Effect of Alternative Accounting Methods

1.

	/	years		
	×			

2.

3.

Inventory Turnover	FIFO Method		LIFO Method	
Cost of Goods Sold		= times*		= times*
Ending Inventory				

*Rounded

4. **Return on Assets**

FIFO/Straight-Line Methods

$$\frac{\text{Net Income}}{\text{Total Assets}} = \underline{\hspace{2cm}} \quad + \quad \underline{\hspace{2cm}} \quad + \quad \underline{\hspace{2cm}} \quad - \quad \underline{\hspace{2cm}}$$

$$= \underline{\hspace{2cm}} = \underline{\hspace{2cm}}$$

LIFO/Double-Declining-Balance Methods

$$= \underline{\hspace{2cm}} \quad + \quad \underline{\hspace{2cm}} \quad + \quad \underline{\hspace{2cm}} \quad - \quad \underline{\hspace{2cm}}$$

$$= \underline{\hspace{2cm}} = \underline{\hspace{2cm}}$$

P12. Corporate Income Statement

1.

2.

APPENDIX A—Working Papers

ACCOUNTING FOR INVESTMENTS

Problems

P1. Trading Securities

1.

		(		×		=		)		
		(		×		=		)		

2.

		(		)		
		(		)		

3.

P2. Methods of Accounting for Long-Term Investments

1.

2.

3.

4.

5.

6.

P3. Long-Term Investments

Unrealized Loss on Long-Term Investments				Allowance to Adjust Long-Term Investments to Market			

P4. Long-Term Investments: Cost-Adjusted-to-Market and Equity Methods

	(		×		)				
	(		×		)				

A-5

P5. Held-to-Maturity Securities

	(	×	/	=	)	

P6. Comprehensive: Accounting for Investments

1. Marsh Service Corporation

a.

b.

c.

Crescent Drilling Company

a.

b.

c.

Logan Oil Field Supplies Company

a.

b.

c.

P6. Comprehensive: Accounting for Investments (Concluded)

2.

		Cost	Market		

3.

4.

(_____ + _____ = _____)

5.

P7. Long-Term Investments: Equity Method

1.

Investment in Waters Corporation*

*Each entry represents 35 percent of either earnings or dividends paid.

2.

3.

4.